NEW YORK

City Highlights

teNeues

Imprint

Texts: Yasemin Erdem
Service: Marianne Bongartz, MaBo-Media, Cologne
Translations: Alphagriese Fachübersetzungen, Dusseldorf; Susanne Olbrich (Service)
Editorial management: Hanna Martin
Layout: Susanne Olbrich, Anne Dörte Schmidt
Imaging and Pre-press: Jan Hausberg, Martin Herterich

Photo credits: Michelle Galindo, Claudia Hehr, Martin Nicholas Kunz, beside: Roland Bauer (pp. 38, 94–95, 98–101); Brooklyn Museum, sculptures by Auguste Rodin (p. 57); courtesy Balthazar (p. 68 t. l.); courtesy Bryant Park Hotel (pp. 116–117); courtesy Chambers Hotel (pp. 126–127); courtesy The Frick Collection (pp. 46–47); courtesy Hotel Gansevoort (pp. 112–113); courtesy Hotel on Rivington, photographers Floto + Warner (pp. 108–109); courtesy The Lowell Hotel (p. 130); courtesy The Lowell Hotel, photographer Karin Kohlberg (p. 131); courtesy Lincoln Center for the Performing Arts (p. 40 t. r.); courtesy The Museum of Modern Art, designed by Yoshio Taniguchi. Night view of The Abby Aldrich Rockefeller Sculpture Garden and The David and Peggy Rockefeller Building. © 2005 Timothy Hursley (pp. 39, 157 l.); courtesy Neue Galerie New York, photographer Claudia Hehr (pp. 54–55); courtesy P.S.1 and artists, photographer Claudia Hehr: Ed McGowin, The Name Change Project, 1970–1972, Mixed media installation (p. 58 o.), OBRA Architects, Jennifer Lee and Pablo Castro, 2006, Beatfuse (p. 59); courtesy Whitney Museum of American Art, Kiki Smith, Blue Girl, 1998, Courtesy PaceWildenstein, New York, photograph by Ellen Page Wilson (p. 48); Gavin Jackson (pp. 106–107, 110–111, 114–115, 118–119, 128–129, 132–133)
Cover: Martin Nicholas Kunz

Content and production: fusion publishing GmbH, Stuttgart . Los Angeles
www.fusion-publishing.com

teNeues Publishing Group

teNeues Verlag GmbH + Co. KG
Am Selder 37
47906 Kempen, Germany
Tel.: 0049 / (0)2152 / 916 0
Fax: 0049 / (0)2152 / 916 111

teNeues Publishing Company
16 West 22nd Street
New York, NY 10010, USA
Tel.: 001-212-627-9090
Fax: 001-212-627-9511

teNeues Publishing UK Ltd.
P.O. Box 402
West Byfleet, KT14 7ZF
Great Britain
Tel.: 0044-1932-403509
Fax: 0044-1932-403514

teNeues France S.A.R.L.
93, rue Bannier
45000 Orléans, France
Tel.: 0033-2-38541071
Fax: 0033-2-38625340

Press department: arehn@teneues.de
Tel.: 0049 / (0)2152 / 916 202

www.teneues.com

The information and facts in this publication have been researched and verified with utmost accuracy. However, the publisher acknowledges that the information may have changed when this work was published and therefore the publisher assumes no liability for the correctness of the information. The editor and publisher make no warranties with respect to the accuracy or completeness of the content of this work, including, without limitation, the "Service" section.

Copy deadline: 1 February 2007

Bibliographic information published by Die Deutsche Bibliothek. Die Deutsche Bibliothek lists this publication in the Deutsche Nationalbibliografie; detailed bibliographic data is available in the Internet at http://dnb.ddb.de.

ISBN 978-3-8327-9193-3

Printed in Italy

Right page:
Empire State Building

Shopping

Hotels

What else?

Service

Left page: View from Top of The Rock, Rockefeller Center
Right page: Left East Village, right Meatpacking District

Island of the Survival Artists

"Ride the wave" is the new motto of our hectic age that demands adaptation on our part. This means taking things as they come and making the best of them. The City of New York is a master at this art of living. More than anywhere else, it teems with both individualists and people who know how to bounce back from adversity. Yet, the spirit of this metropolis is proud and dignified. The best example of this is September 11, 2001: it was an unfathomable tragedy, but the city has risen from it like a phoenix from the ashes.

The clocks tick faster here than in other places. Everything seems restless, occasionally hectic, but also wonderfully flowing and dynamic. Countless skyscrapers tower up into the air, and the dreams that this city provokes are just as large. Some are fulfilled, others not. Even if

New Yorkers sometimes complain about their city, they love it and are loyal to it—at least most of them. For the others, it may be a temporary stage in life, a springboard that is certain to remain unforgettable. New York gets under your skin and makes you tougher. It educates you. It's heated and cold, crazy, and creative—an island of immigrants, pioneers, and (survival) artists.

Not only dreams but also traditions are a part of life here. The name "Little Italy" keeps its promise: a small piece of Italy, even if it's located north of Chinatown. People from the most diverse backgrounds peacefully coexist in this city without much competition against each other. New York is also an island in this sense. A place that is almost too good to be true.

Left page: Left Midtown Westside, right Rockefeller Center
Right page: View of Downtown from Brooklyn

L' île des artistes de la vie

« Ride the wave » – C'est le slogan de notre époque nerveuse qui exige toujours des adaptations. Ce qui veut dire qu'il faut prendre les choses comme elles viennent et en tirer ce qu'il y a de mieux. Il faut donc « aller avec la vague ». C'est exactement ce qui caractérise la ville de New York par excellence. Nulle part ailleurs, il n'y a tant d'individualistes et de poussahs, l'esprit de la métropole est fier et digne. Le meilleur exemple est le 11 septembre 2001 : une tragédie incroyable, mais la ville en est sortie comme phénix renaissant de ses cendres.

Les horloges vont plus vite ici qu'ailleurs, tout semble rapide, même agité mais en même temps merveilleusement fluide et dynamique. De nombreux gratte-ciels s'érigent en même temps vers le ciel, tout aussi grands sont les rêves qui sont générés par cette ville. Certains se réalisent, d'autres pas. Même s'il arrive aux new-yorkais de se plaindre de leur ville, ils l'aiment et lui restent fidèles. Au moins le plus souvent. Pour tous les autres, elle peut être une étape transitoire de leur vie, un tremplin qui pourtant reste inoubliable. Parce que New York vous marque. Vous endurcit. Vous éduque. C'est chaud et froid, fou et créatif. Une île d'immigrés, de pionniers et d'artistes en survie.

Ici, on ne vit pas que de rêves mais aussi de traditions. Ainsi Little Italy tient ses promesses : un petit morceau d'Italie même s'il est situé un peu au nord de Chinatown. Des gens d'origine les plus diverses cohabitent paisiblement sans se faire concurrence. En ce sens, New York est aussi une île. Un endroit presque trop beau pour être réel.

Left page: Louis Vuitton on Fifth Avenue
Right page: Left Financial District, right Times Square

La isla de los artistas de la vida

"Ride the Wave" es el nuevo lema de nuestra frenética época, que requiere constante adaptación. Es decir, tomar las cosas tal y como vienen, y sacar el mejor provecho de ellas. Simplemente "cabalgar sobre la ola", el estilo de vida que es perfectamente personificado por la ciudad de Nueva York. En ningún otro lugar, se encuentran tantas personas individualistas y ambiciosas y por eso, el espíritu de la metrópoli es tan orgulloso y digno. El mejor ejemplo es el 11 de septiembre de 2001: una tragedia inconcebible, desde la cual la ciudad ha sabido resurgir como ave Fénix de sus cenizas.

Aquí, los relojes corren más de prisa que en otros lugares, todo parece ser en movimiento perpetuo, a veces frenético, pero a la vez maravillosamente fluido y dinámico. Los sueños que la ciudad inspira son tan formidables como sus incontables rascacielos que se alzan hacia el cielo ... algunos se realizan, otros quién sabe. A pesar de quejarse de ella de vez en cuando, los neoyorkinos aman su ciudad y son fieles a ella. Al menos en la mayoría de los casos. En la vida de los demás, podría representar una estación de paso, un trampolín, pero lo cierto es que nunca se olvidará. Porque Nueva York endurece, fortalece y enriquece, es ardiente y álgida, loca, creativa, una isla para los inmigrantes, los pioneros y los artistas (de la vida).

Se viven sueños, y también tradiciones. Little Italy cumple con lo que su nombre promete: un pedacito de Italia, aunque sea ... al norte de Chinatown. Gente de origen heterogéneo coexiste en la ciudad, más pacíficamente aquí que en otros lugares. También en este sentido Nueva York es una isla. Un lugar casi demasiado bello para ser verdad.

Left page: Shopping in SoHo
Right page: View of Central Park

L'isola degli artisti della vita

"Ride the wave" – è questo il nuovo motto della nostra epoca, fatta di frenesia e costante adeguamento. Come dire, prendere quello che viene, e trarne il meglio. "Cavalcare l'onda", appunto. Esattamente l'atmosfera che regna sovrana nella città di New York. In nessun'altro luogo al mondo si ammassano tanto individualismo e tanta ambizione, e allo stesso tempo la metropoli dimostra il suo spirito orgoglioso e fiero. L'esempio migliore è l'11 settembre 2001: una tragedia inconcepibile, dalle quale la città ha saputo risorgere come una fenice dalle sue ceneri.

Qui gli orologi vanno più rapidi che nel resto del mondo, tutto è in perenne movimento, talvolta al limite della frenesia, ma allo stesso tempo meravigliosamente fluido e dinamico. La città ispira sogni che si protendono al cielo come i suoi innumerevoli grattacieli ... alcuni si avverano, altri chissà. Anche se a volte i newyorkesi si lamentano della propria città, la amano e le sono fedeli. Bè, quasi sempre. Per tutti gli altri potrà essere una fermata intermedia, un trampolino di lancio, ma di certo non resterà dimenticata. Perché New York tempra, plasma, insegna, è bollente e gelida, creativa, un'isola per emigranti, pionieri e artisti (della vita).

E così come i sogni, si vivono anche le tradizioni. Little Italy mantiene ciò che il nome promette: uno spicchio di Italia, e non importa che si trovi al nord di Chinatown. Genti delle più svariate origini coesistono nella città, più pacificamente qui che altrove. Anche in questo senso New York è un'isola. Un posto quasi troppo bello per esistere davvero.

Sightseeing

New York offers such an abundance of sights that you have to set your priorities. If possible, you should connect them with a fixed route that you can let yourself wander along such as from Central Park to the southern tip of Manhattan. Among the "musts" are Ground Zero, the famous museums, the Statue of Liberty, Brooklyn Bridge, Grand Central Station, and the harbor area in which the history of the city once began.

New York offre une telle richesse de curiosité qu'il faut en définir les priorités. Il faut si possible, les assimiler à un parcours fixe sur lequel on se laisse aller, par exemple du Central Park jusqu'au point sud de Manhattan. Les « Must » sont le Ground Zero, les musées célèbres, la Statue de la Liberté, Brooklyn Bridge, Grand Central Station et les alentours du port, où commença jadis l'histoire de la ville.

Nueva York ofrece tanta abundancia de oportunidades, que es necesario establecerse prioridades. Posiblemente enlazadas a través de una ruta fija, por ejemplo desde el Central Park hasta el extremo sur de Manhattan. Imprescindible es la Zona Cero, los célebres Museos, la Estatua de la Libertad, el Puente de Brooklyn, la Gran Estación Central y también el distrito del puerto, origen de la historia de la ciudad.

I luoghi che vale la pena vedere a New York sono così tanti che è necessario stabilire delle priorità, magari riunite nello stesso itinerario, per esempio dal Central Park fino alla punta sud di Manhattan. Tra i "must" troviamo sicuramente Ground Zero, i famosi Musei, la Statua della Libertà, il Ponte di Brooklyn, Grand Central Station e il distretto portuale: in fondo, è da qui che iniziò la storia della città.

Left page: Chrysler Building
Right page: Left Times Square, right Saint Patrick's Cathedral

Left page: Top left City Hall, top right Wall Street, New York Stock Exchange, bottom UN Headquarters
Right page: Top Ellis Island, bottom view of the Hearst Headquarters from Top of the Rock, Rockefeller Center

Statue of Liberty

Liberty Island
New York, NY 10004
Phone: +1 / 212 / 3 63 32 00
www.nps.gov/stli

Opening hours: Daily 9.30 am to 5 pm/8.30 pm (holiday periods)
Admission: Ferry adults $ 11.50, children (4–12) $ 4.50, senior citizens $ 9.50; "Time Pass" reservations are required to enter the statue, available free from the ferry company or online
Public transportation: 1 South Ferry; R, W Whitehall Street; Ferry Battery Park
Map: No. 48
Editor's tip: Avoid the crowds. Just take the boat to Ellis Island or the Staten Island ferry and enjoy the view from the water.

Miss Liberty has greeted immigrants and tourists in the harbor of New York since 1886. The sculpture, which weighs 225 t and is covered with copper, was a gift from the French Republic. Donations financed the base. Gustave Eiffel, the builder of the Eiffel Tower in Paris, constructed the supporting steel scaffolding of the 150-foot high statue.

« Miss liberty » accueille des immigrants et touristes dans le port de New York depuis 1886. La sculpture d'un poids de 225 t, couverte de cuivre était un cadeau de la République Française, le socle a été financé par des dons. Gustave Eiffel, le constructeur de la Tour Eiffel à Paris a construit l'échafaudage portant la statue qui a une hauteur de 46 m en acier.

"Doña Libertad" da la bienvenida a inmigrantes y turistas en el puerto de Nueva York desde 1886. La escultura mide 46 m, pesa 225 t y está recubierta de cobre; es un regalo de la República Francesa, mientras que su base fue financiada por donaciones. La estructura de soporte es de Gustave Eiffel, el constructor de la Torre Eiffel de Paris.

La "Signora Libertà" dà il benvenuto a immigranti e turisti nel porto di New York dal 1886. La scultura è alta 46 m, pesa 225 t ed è ricoperta in rame; fu donata della Repubblica Francese, mentre la base fu finanziata tramite donazioni. Gustave Eiffel, autore della Torre Eiffel di Parigi, costruì l'armatura portante in acciaio.

World Trade Center Site / Ground Zero

West Street Highway / Liberty Street / Church Street / Vesey Street
Midtown
www.wtcsitememorial.org

Opening hours: Only accessible on a tour. Exhibition and tours can be booked at: www.tributenyc.org
Public transportation: A, C Chambers Street-WTC; E World Trade Center
Map: No. 54
Editor's tip: Firemen, survivors and relatives of the victims conduct daily the Tribute Center Walking Tour. Start: Tribute Center, 120 Liberty Street. Reservations: www.telecharge.com under "other events".

A large pit where the World Trade Center once stood is still a reminder of the terrorist attacks of September 11, 2001. Based on an idea by Daniel Libeskind, the foundation stone for the Freedom Tower was laid on July 4, 2004. Its inscription is dedicated to the victims of the attack. Construction is also in progress on a light-flooded underground subway station.

Le World Trade Center se trouvait avant, une fosse rappelle toujours les attaques terroristes du 11 septembre 2001. Le 4 juillet 2004, la première pierre a été posée pour le Freedom Tower suivant une idée de Daniel Libeskind. Son inscription est dédiée aux victimes de l'attentat. En plus, une station de métro souterraine, remplie de lumière est en construction.

Allí donde estaba el World Trade Center, un enorme agujero queda en memoria de los ataques del 11 de Septiembre de 2001. Las bases de la Torre de la Libertad, idea de Daniel Libeskind, fueron sentadas el 4 de Julio de 2004, y lleva una inscripción dedicada a las víctimas. Al lado está en construcción una estación de metro inundada de luz.

Là dove si ergeva il World Trade Center, un'enorme fossa rimane a ricordare l'attacco terroristico dell'11 settembre 2001. La prima pietra della Freedom Tower, nata da un'idea di Daniel Libeskind, è stata posata il 4 luglio 2004, e porta un'inscrizione dedicata alle vittime dell'attacco. Nei pressi è in costruzione una luminosissima stazione sotterranea della metropolitana.

Brooklyn Bridge

East River
Lower East Side / Brooklyn

Public transportation: 4, 5, 6, J, M, Z Brooklyn Bridge-City Hall;
A, C High Street
Map: No. 6
Editor's tip: The nicest walk is towards Manhattan: take the subway line A or C to High Street Station.

The construction of the Brooklyn Bridge wrote architectural history. John Augustus Roebling began construction work on the suspension bridge that connects Brooklyn with Manhattan in 1869. A footpath and bikeway run above the roadway across the East River, which offers an impressive view of the skyline.

La construction du Brooklyn Bridge est entrée dans l'histoire de l'architecture. En 1869, John Augustus Roebling commençait avec les travaux de ce pont suspendu qui relie le quartier Brooklyn avec Manhattan. Au-dessus de la route, un chemin réservé aux piétons et aux vélos traverse le East River qui offre une vue impressionnante sur la silhouette des gratte-ciels.

La construcción del Puente de Brooklyn escribió la historia de la arquitectura. John Augustus Roebling empezó en 1869 las obras para el puente colgante que une Brooklyn y Manhattan atravesando el East River. Por encima de la carretera se encuentra una vía para peatones y bicicletas que brinda una vista inmejorable del perfil de la ciudad.

La costruzione del Ponte di Brooklyn ha scritto la storia dell'architettura. John Augustus Roebling inziò nel 1869 i lavori per il ponte sospeso che unisce i quartieri di Brooklyn e Manhattan attraversando l'East River. Al di sopra della carreggiata stradale corre una via pedonale e ciclabile che offre un'impareggiabile vista dello skyline.

Grand Central Terminal

15 Vanderbilt Avenue, Hall 2A
New York, NY 10017
Midtown
Phone: +1 / 212 / 3 40 23 45
www.grandcentralterminal.com

Opening hours: 5.30 am to 1.30 am, shops Mon–Fri 8 am to 8 pm, Sat 10 am to 8 pm, Sun 11 am to 6 pm
Admission: Free access, guided tours per person $ 5
Public transportation: 4, 5, 6, 7, MTA Subway 42 Street-Grand Central
Map: No. 22

The main hall of New York's largest station is larger than the nave of any church. In addition to classy restaurants like the famous "Oyster Bar" and many other places to eat, the stylish building—which was officially opened in 1913—houses about 50 stores. The halls are also used to hold events and exhibitions on a regular basis.

La salle principale de la plus grande gare de New York est plus grande que n'importe quel nef d'église. En plus, des restaurants nobles comme le très connu « Oyster Bar » et de nombreux autres endroits pour manger, ce bâtiment, inauguré en 1913, héberge environ 50 magasins. D'ailleurs, les salles sont régulièrement utilisées pour des événements et expositions.

El salón principal de la estación más grande de Nueva York supera la nave de cualquier iglesia. Además de locales refinados como el famoso "Oyster Bar" y varias otras opciones gastronómicas, el elegante edificio, inaugurado en 1913, acoge alrededor de 50 tiendas. Los salones suelen ser utilizados también para exhibiciones y otras actividades.

La sala maggiore della più grande stazione di New York supera la navata di qualsiasi chiesa. Oltre a locali raffinati come il famoso "Oyster Bar" e numerosi altri punti di ristorazione, l'elegante edificio, inaugurato nel 1913, ospita circa 50 negozi. Le sale vengono regolarmente usate anche per esibizioni e altri eventi.

Times Square

42nd Street / Broadway
Midtown
www.timessquare.com

Attractions: Broadway and off Broadway theaters, big flagship stores and illuminated advertising
Public transportation: 1, 2, 3, A, C, E, N, R, S, W, Q 42 Street-Times Square
Map: No. 51
Editor's tip: Tickets for Broadway shows on the same day are available at TKTS booths at up to 50 % off full-price (Broadway, corner 47th Street).

The most famous intersection of New York was renamed in 1904 after the "New York Times", which had its publishing headquarters there. Since the end of the 19th century, Times Square has been the hub of the New York entertainment district. With its countless resident record companies, the area is also the center for the music business.

Le carrefour le plus connu de New York a été renommé en 1904 d'après le « New York Times » qui y possédait ses bureaux d'édition. Depuis la fin du XIXe siècle, le Times Square est le centre du quartier de divertissement de New York. Avec d'innombrables maisons de disques, ce quartier est aussi le centre du marché de la musique.

El cruce más famoso de Nueva York debe su nombre desde 1904 al "New York Times", cuya sede editorial se encontraba entonces allí. Times Square representa desde los finales del siglo XIX el centro del barrio del entretenimiento de Nueva York, con sus numerosas casas discográficas es también el centro de la industria musical.

Il più noto crocevia di New York prese il suo nome nel 1904 dal "New York Times", la cui sede editoriale vi si trovava allora. Times Square costituisce sin dalla fine del secolo XIX il centro del quartiere del divertimento newyorkese. E con le innumerevoli case discografiche che là si sono stabilite, la zona è anche il centro dell'industria musicale.

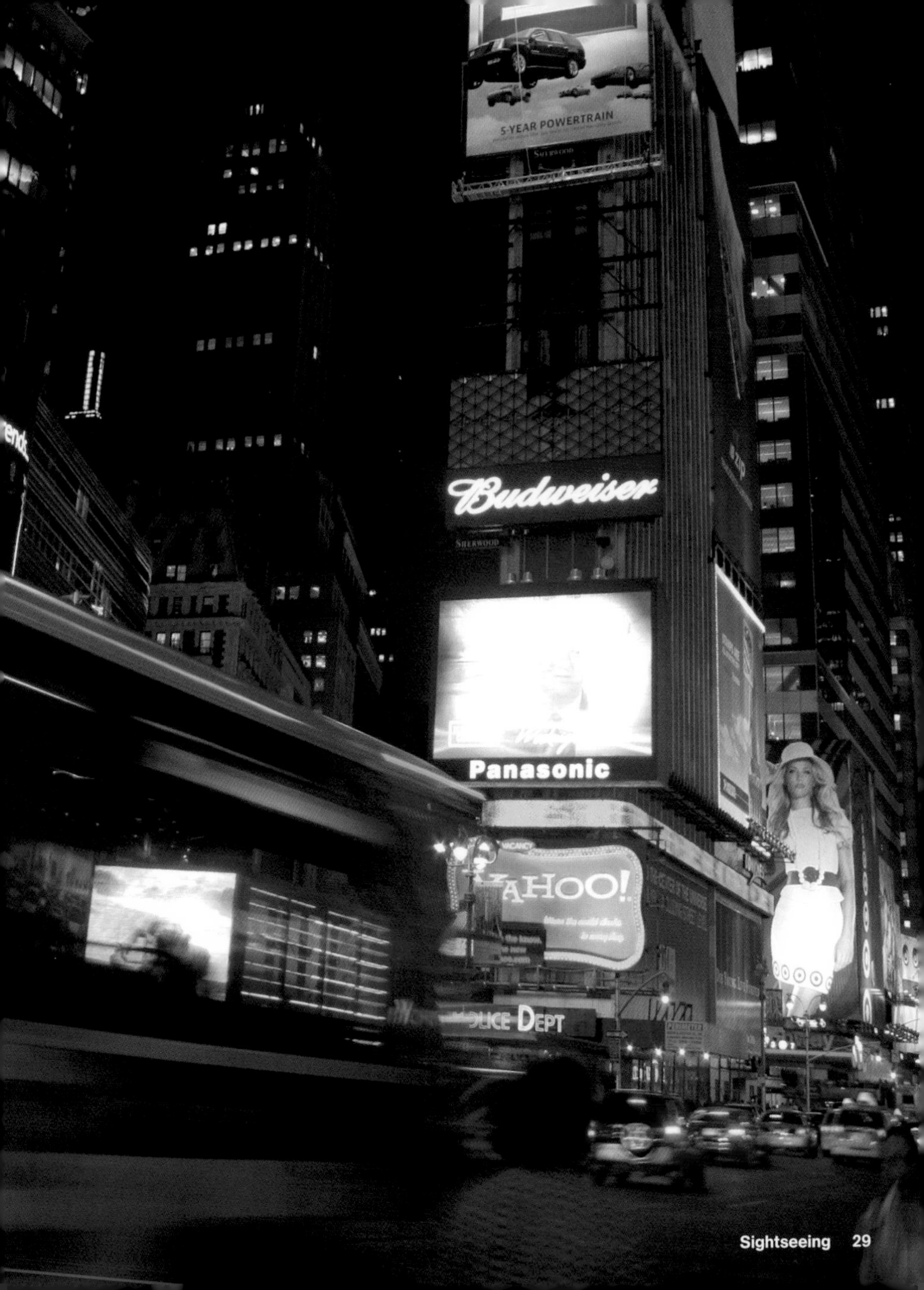
5-YEAR POWERTRAIN
Budweiser
SHERWOOD
Panasonic

Top of the Rock Observation Deck Rockefeller Center

30 Rockefeller Plaza
New York, NY 10112
Midtown
Phone: +1 / 212 / 6 98 20 00
www.topoftherocknyc.com

Opening hours: Daily 8 am to midnight, last elevator 11 pm
Admission: $ 17.50, children (6–12) $ 11.25, senior citizens
(62 and over) $ 16, reservations recommended
Public transportation: B, D, F, V 47–50 Street-Rockefeller Center
Map: No. 52

With its 21 high-rises, this largest private business and entertainment complex in the world is a little city within the metropolis. The General Electric Building includes both the legendary "Rainbow Room" restaurant and the Top of the Rock Observation Deck, which was reopened in 2005.

Le plus grand complexe privé d'affaires et de divertissements du monde est une petite ville dans la ville et consiste en 21 gratte-ciels. Dans le General Electric Building, se trouvent le restaurant légendaire « Rainbow Room » et la plate-forme d'observation Top of the Rock réouverte en 2005.

El centro de negocios y ocio privado más grande del mundo, con sus 21 rascacielos, representa una pequeña ciudad dentro de la propia ciudad. En el edificio de la General Electric se encuentran también el legendario restaurante "Rainbow Room" y el mirador Top of the Rock, reabierto en el año 2005.

Il più grande centro privato d'affari e di svago al mondo, con i suoi 21 grattacieli, rappresenta una piccola città nella città. Nell'edificio della General Electric si trovano inoltre il leggendario ristorante "Rainbow Room" e la piatta-forma panoramica Top of the Rock, riaperta al pubblico nel 2005.

Culture
Museums Galleries Theaters Cinemas

New York has more art treasures to offer than any other city: there are more than 60 museums in Manhattan alone, plus a lively and dynamic art scene with many galleries, cultural centers, and artists' houses. High culture and alternative art exist peacefully next to each other here with room for the creative talents of every population group.

New York a plus de trésors d'art à offrir que toute autre ville : Rien qu'à Manhattan, on trouve plus de 60 musées, plus un milieu artistique dynamique et vivant avec de nombreuses galeries, des centres culturels et des maisons d'artistes. Ici, la haute culture et l'art alternatif coexistent en paix et il existe également une place pour les talents créatifs de chaque groupe de la population.

Nueva York es una ciudad rica en tesoros artísticos, incomparable a ninguna otra: solamente en Manhattan hay 60 museos, la escena artística es intrigante y dinámica, con incontable galerías, centros culturales y casas de arte. Elevada cultura y arte alternativo coexisten felizmente, siendo los talentos creativos presentes en todas las culturas.

New York è ricca di tesori artistici come nessun'altra città: solo a Manhattan ci sono più di 60 musei, e una scena artistica intrigante e dinamica con innumerevoli gallerie, centri culturali e case d'arte. Cultura superiore e arte alternativa vanno amichevolmente a braccetto, e troviamo talenti creativi di tutte le provenienze etniche e culturali.

Left page: Metropolitan Museum of Art
Right page: Left Chelsea Galleries, right Brooklyn Museum

The Skyscraper Museum

39 Battery Place
New York, NY 10280
Battery Park City
Phone: +1 / 212 / 9 68 19 61
www.skyscraper.org

Opening hours: Wed–Sun noon to 6 pm
Admission: $ 5, children, students, senior citizens $ 2.50
Public transportation: 1 South Ferry; R, W Whitehall Street;
4, 5 Bowling Green; J, M, Z Broad Street
Map: No. 45

America invented the high-rise—and New York became an architectural mountain range over time: increasingly more breathtaking buildings rose up into the sky. The Skyscraper Museum in Battery Park City documents this development and demonstrates the various constructions of skyscrapers.

L'amérique a inventé les gratte-ciels – et avec le temps, New York est devenu une montagne architecturale : De plus en plus de bâtiments étonnants se sont élevés vers le ciel. Le Skyscraper Museum à Battery Park City confirme ce développement et montre les différentes constructions des gratte-ciels.

América inventó los pisos altos –y con el paso del tiempo Nueva York se convirtió en una cordillera arquitectónica: más y más construcciones imponentes se elevan hacia el cielo. El Skyscraper Museum en Battery Park City refleja este desarrollo, y enseña los diferentes diseños de rascacielos.

L'America ha inventato i piani alti ... e New York si è trasformata nel tempo in una catena montuosa architettonica: sono sempre più gli edifici mozzafiato che si proiettano verso il cielo. Lo Skyscraper Museum di Battery Park City documenta questo sviluppo, ed espone inoltre le diverse costruzioni dei vari grattacieli.

The Museum of Modern Art / MoMA

11 West 53 Street
New York, NY 10019
Midtown
Phone: +1 / 212 / 7 08 94 00
www.moma.org

Opening hours: Wed+Thu and Sat–Mon 10.30 am to 5.30 pm,
Fri 10.30 am to 8 pm, Tue closed
Admission: $ 20, students $ 12, senior citizens (65 and over) $ 16,
children (16 and under) free
Public transportation: E, V Fifth Avenue-53 Street;
B, D, F 47–50 Streets-Rockefeller Center
Map: No. 37

This collection of modern art is legendary:
150,000 exhibits of art, photography, architecture, and design are shown in alternation.
These include works by Pablo Picasso, Henri
Matisse, and Joseph Beuys. The building,
which was redesigned by Yoshio Taniguchi, is
an artwork in its own right. When you enter
the more than 100-foot tall atrium, it takes
your breath away.

Cette collection d'art moderne est légendaire.
150 000 objets en provenance de l'art, la
photographie, l'architecture et le design sont
exposés en alternance dont des œuvres de
Pablo Picasso, Henri Matisse et Joseph Beuys.
Le bâtiment, refaçonné par Yoshio Taniguchi
est une œuvre d'art en lui-même. Le visiteur
qui entre est stupéfait par le patio qui a une
hauteur de 33 m.

Su colección de arte moderno es legendaria: la
exposición alterna 150 000 obras de arte, foto-
grafía, arquitectura y diseño, incluso obras de
Pablo Picasso, Henri Matisse e Joseph Beuys. El
mismo edificio es una obra de arte, moldeado
por Yoshio Taniguchi. Su entrada, con sus 33 m
de altura, quita el aliento.

Collezione leggendaria d'arte moderna: vi si
espongono a rotazione 150 000 lavori d'arte,
fotografia, architettura e design, tra cui opere
di Pablo Picasso, Henri Matisse e Joseph Beuys.
Lo stesso edificio è un'opera d'arte, trasformata da Yoshio Taniguchi. L'ingresso all'atrio
toglie il fiato al visitatore, grazie ai suoi 33 m
di altezza.

Lincoln Center for the Performing Arts

140 West 65th Street
New York, NY 10023
Lincoln Square
Phone: +1 / 212 / 8 75 54 56
www.lincolncenter.org

Opening hours: According to venue
Admission: According to event
Public transportation: 1 66 Street-Lincoln Center; 1, A, B, C, D
59 Street-Columbus Circle
Map: No. 30

The largest cultural center in the world with its seven concert halls and theaters offers seats for audiences of up to 15,000 people. In 1961, some scenes for "West Side Story" were filmed in the quarter, which seemed like a slum at that time. The three buildings of the Metropolitan Opera, Avery Fisher Hall, and New York State Theater are arranged around a large plaza.

Le plus grand centre culturel du monde a sept salles de concerts et théâtres et offre de la place à 15 000 spectateurs. En 1961, des scènes de la « West Side Story » ont été tournées dans ce quartier qui, à l'époque, ressemblait à un bidonville. Les trois bâtiments Metropolitan Opéra, Avery Fisher Hall et New York State Theater se regroupent autour d'une large place.

El más amplio centro cultural del mundo ofrece hasta 15 000 lugares en sus siete salas de conciertos y teatros. En 1961 se rodaron unas escenas de "West Side Story" en el entonces gueto de muy mala fama. Metropolitan Opera, Avery Fisher Hall y New York State Theater se concentran alrededor de una amplia plaza.

Il più vasto centro culturale al mondo può ospitare fino a 15 000 spettatori nelle sue sette sale da concerto e teatri. Nel 1961 alcune scene di "West Side Story" furono girate nel quartiere, al tempo squallido e malfamato. I tre edifici Metropolitan Opera, Avery Fisher Hall e New York State Theater circondano un'ampio piazzale.

American Museum of Natural History

Central Park West / 79th Street
New York, NY 10024
Upper West Side
Phone: +1 / 212 / 7 69 51 00
www.amnh.org

Opening hours: Daily 10 am to 5.45 pm
Admission: $ 14, senior citizens, students $ 11, children (12 and under) $ 8
Public transportation: B, C 81 Street-Museum of Natural History; 1 79 Street-Broadway
Map: No. 2

With more than 35 million exhibits, this is one of the three largest natural history museums in the world. The biology of human beings and animals is demonstrated here, with a focus on the native peoples and the flora and fauna of America. Also worth seeing: the Hayden Planetarium, the Imax Cinema, the Space Theater, and the Big Bang Theater.

Avec plus de 35 millions d'objets exposés, c'est un des trois plus grands musées d'histoire naturelle du monde. Ici on montre la biologie de l'homme et des animaux avec une concentration sur les peuples primitifs, la flore et la faune de l'Amérique du Nord. A voir aussi : le Hayden Planetarium, le cinéma Imax, le Space Theater et le Big Bang Theater.

Es uno de los tres mayores museos de historia natural del mundo, con más de 35 millones de ejemplares. Enseña la biología de hombres y animales, enfocando en las civilizaciones, la flora y la fauna nativas americanas. También para ver: Hayden Planetarium, cine Imax, Space Theater y Big Bang Theater.

Con oltre 35 milioni di pezzi in esposizione, è fra i tre maggiori musei di storia naturale al mondo. Mostra la biologia di esseri umani e animali, con particolare attenzione ai nativi americani e alla flora e fauna indigena. Da vedere anche: Hayden Planetarium, cinema Imax, Space Theater e Big Bang Theater.

The Frick Collection

1 East 70th Street
New York, NY 10021
Upper East Side
Phone: +1 / 212 / 2 88 07 00
www.frick.org

Opening hours: Tue–Sat 10 am to 6 pm, Sun 11 am to 5 pm, Mon closed
Admission: $ 15, senior citizens (62 and over) $ 10, students $ 5, Sun 11 am to 1 pm pay what you wish
Public transportation: 6 68 Street-Hunter College
Map: No. 21

As one of the most significant art collectors of the USA, the steel magnate Henry Clay Frick acquired works of the great painters from the 14th to the 19th century. He also collected precious furniture from the epochs of Louis XV and Louis XVI, as well as valuable porcelain. He had a city palace built on Fifth Avenue, which has served as a museum since 1935.

En tant qu'un des collectionneurs d'art les plus importants des Etats-Unis, l'industriel de l'acier Henry Clay Frick a acquis des œuvres de grands peintres du XIVe au XIXe siècle et des meubles précieux des époques Louis XV et Louis XVI ainsi que de la porcelaine de haute valeur. Il a fait construire un palais urbain dans la Cinquième Avenue qui sert de musée depuis 1935.

Uno de los mayores coleccionistas de arte en Estados Unidos, el magnate del acero Henry Clay Frick reunió obras de los principales pintores de los siglos de XIV a XIX, preciados muebles de los períodos Luís XV y XVI y valiosas porcelanas. El palacio que hizo construir en la Quinta Avenida es museo desde 1935.

Tra i più importanti collezionisti d'arte degli Stati Uniti, il magnate dell'acciaio Henry Clay Frick acquisì opere dei più grandi pittori dal secolo XIV al XIX, oltre a preziosi mobili delle epoche Luigi XV e Luigi XVI e a pregiate porcellane. Il palazzo che fece costruire sulla Fifth Avenue funge da museo dal 1935.

Whitney Museum of American Art

945 Madison Avenue
New York, NY 10021
Upper East Side
Phone: +1 / 212 / 5 70 36 76
www.whitney.org

Opening hours: Wed+Thu, Sat+Sun 11 am to 6 pm, Fri 1 pm to 9 pm, Mon+Tue closed
Admission: $ 15, students, senior citizens (62 and over) $ 10, Fri 6 pm to 9 pm pay what you wish
Public transportation: 6 77 Street
Map: No. 53

In 1931, the art patron Gertrude Vanderbilt Whitney established a studio museum—with her private collection as the basis—in order to offer a platform for American art, which had been largely ignored up to that time. The current museum on Madison Avenue holds one of the most important collections of contemporary American art.

En 1931, la mécène d'art Gertrude Vanderbilt Whitney a crée – avec sa collection privée comme base – un musée de studio pour offrir une plate-forme à l'art américain, encore peu connu à l'époque. Le musée d'aujourd'hui dans l'Avenue Madison possède une des plus importantes collections de l'art américain contemporain.

En 1931 la mecenas Gertrude Vanderbilt Whitney fundó un estudio-museo comenzando por su colección privada, para dar a conocer el arte americano, hasta entonces muy poco considerado. Hoy en día el edificio en la avenida Madison acoge una de las más importantes colecciones de arte americano contemporáneo.

Nel 1931 la mecenate Gertrude Vanderbilt Whitney fondò un museo-studio a partire dalla propria collezione privata, per dare visibilità all'arte americana, che fino a quel tempo era stata generalmente ignorata. L'odierno edificio sulla Madison Avenue ospita una delle più importanti collezioni d'arte americana contemporanea.

The Metropolitan Museum of Art

1000 Fifth Avenue /
82nd Street
New York, NY 10028
Upper East Side
Phone: +1 / 212 / 5 35 77 10
www.metmuseum.org

Opening hours: Tue–Thu 9.30 am to 5.30 pm, Fri+Sat 9.30 am to
9 pm, Sun to 5.30 pm, Mon closed
Admission: $ 20, students, senior citizens (65 and over) $ 10,
children (12 and under) free
Public transportation: 4, 5, 6 86 Street-Lexington Avenue;
B, C 86 Street-Central Park West
Map: No. 35
Editor's tip: You can visit "The Cloisters" in north Manhattan with
the entry ticket to The Metropolitan Museum on the same day.

The Metropolitan Museum, established in
1870, is considered one of the most significant art museums in the world. It possesses
more than two million exhibits. The perma-
nent exhibition is supplemented by special
exhibitions on individual artists or epochs on
a regular basis. The displays include European,
American, Egyptian, and Asian art.

Le Metropolitan Museum est un des musées
d'art les plus importants du monde. Il a été
fondé en 1870. Il possède plus deux millions
d'objets, l'exposition permanente est régulièrement complétée par des expositions spéciales
sur certains artistes ou époques. Ici on voit,
entre autres, del'art européen, américain,
égyptien et asiatique.

Fundado en 1870, el Metropolitan Museum es
uno de los museos de arte más importantes
del mundo, con sus más de dos millones de
ejemplares. Además de obras en exposición
continua hay exposiciones temporales sobre
artistas o épocas específicas. Entre otras, es
posible admirar obras de arte europeo, americano, egipcio y asiático.

Fondato nel 1870, il Metropolitan Museum è
annoverato tra i più importanti musei d'arte
al mondo, ospitando oltre due milioni di pezzi.
Le opere in esposizione permanente sono
regolarmente affiancate da mostre speciali a
tema, su artisti o epoche specifiche. Tra l'altro,
vi si ammira arte europea, americana, egizia e
asiatica.

Neue Galerie New York

1048 Fifth Avenue
New York, NY 10028
Upper East Side
Phone: +1 / 212 / 6 28 62 00
www.neuegalerie.org

Opening hours: Mon, Thu, Sat+Sun 11 am to 6 pm, Fri to 9 pm, Tue+Wed closed
Admission: $ 15, students, senior citizens $ 10, children (12 and under) not admitted
Public transportation: 4, 5, 6 86 Street-Lexington Avenue; B, C 86 Street-Central Park West
Map: No. 38
Editor's tip: You can see the most expensive painting ever sold ($ 135 million) – Adele Bloch-Bauer I by Gustav Klimt.

The Neue Galerie is dedicated to German and Austrian art. In addition to works by Gustav Klimt, Oskar Kokoschka, Josef Hoffmann, and Otto Wagner, it has paintings by the groups of "The Blue Rider" and "The Bridge", as well as representatives of the Bauhaus School. Also in the building: "Café Sabarsky" with Viennese coffee specialties.

La Neue Galerie est consacrée à l'art allemand et autrichien. A côté des œuvres de Gustav Klimt, Oskar Kokoscha, Josef Hoffmann et Otto Wagner, on trouve ici des travaux des groupes « Le Cavalier Bleu » et « Le Pont » et des représentants de l'école du Bauhaus. Dans la maison aussi : le « Café Sabarsky » avec des spécialités de café viennoises.

La Neue Galerie está dedicada al arte alemán y austriaco. Además de obras de Gustav Klimt, Oskar Kokoschka, Josef Hoffmann y Otto Wagner es posible encontrar trabajos de los conjuntos artísticos "El Jinete Azul" y "El Puente" y de representantes de la escuela de la Bauhaus, y el "Café Sabarsky" con sus especialidades vienesas.

La Neue Galerie è dedicata all'arte tedesca e austriaca. Oltre a opere di Gustav Klimt, Oskar Kokoschka, Josef Hoffmann e Otto Wagner, vi si posso trovare lavori dei gruppi artistici "Il Cavaliere Azzurro" e "Il Ponte" e di rappresentanti della scuola Bauhaus. All'interno anche il "Café Sabarsky" con specialità viennesi.

Brooklyn Museum

200 Eastern Parkway
Brooklyn, NY 11238
Phone: +1 / 718 / 6 38 50 00
www.brooklynmuseum.org

Opening hours: Wed–Fri 10 am to 5 pm, Sat+Sun 11 am to 6 pm,
Mon+Tue closed, first Sat of each month to 11 pm
Admission: $ 8, students, senior citizens (65 and over) $ 4,
children (12 and under) free
Public transportation: 2, 3 Eastern Parkway-Brooklyn Museum
Map: No. 7

This museum has one of the biggest art collections in the USA. The Egyptian collection is considered one of the most significant in the world. The Pre-Columbian collection explores an unknown world. Masterpieces of American art—such as the "Brooklyn Bridge" by Georgia O'Keeffe—are represented here, as well as 58 sculptures by Auguste Rodin.

Le musée possède une des plus grandes collections d'art des Etats-Unis. La collection égyptienne compte parmi les plus importantes du monde et la collection précolombienne ouvre un monde inconnu. Des chefs d'œuvre de l'art des USA – comme le « Pont de Brooklyn » de Georgia O'Keeffe – sont représentés ici, ainsi que 58 sculptures d'Auguste Rodin.

Este museo reúne una de las mayores colecciones de arte de Estados Unidos. La colección egipcia es una de las más importantes del mundo, y la precolombina explora un universo poco conocido. Hay obras maestras de arte americano como el "Brooklyn Bridge" de Georgia O'Keeffe, y 58 esculturas de Auguste Rodin.

Il museo ospita una delle maggiori collezioni d'arte degli Stati Uniti. La collezione egizia è considerata una delle più importanti del globo, e la precolombiana esplora un mondo poco conosciuto. Vi si espongono capolavori dell'arte americana come il "Brooklyn Bridge" di Georgia O'Keeffe e 58 sculture di Auguste Rodin.

P.S.1 Contemporary Art Center

22—25 Jackson Avenue
Long Island City, NY 11101
Queens
Phone: +1 / 718 / 7 84 20 84
www.ps1.org

Opening hours: Thu—Mon noon to 6 pm
Admission: $ 5, students, senior citizens $ 2
Public transportation: E, V 23 Street-Ely Avenue; 7 45 Road-
Court Square; G 21 Street-Van Alst
Map: No. 41

The entire complex of this art center in Queens—a former elementary school—is endowed with works of art from the garden to the roof terrace. The museum shop is considered a lucrative treasure chest. DJs play music at warm-up events on the weekend and culinary specialties of various cultural groups are offered here.

Tout le complexe de centre d'art dans le Queens – une ex-école primaire – est muni d'œuvres d'art du jardin jusqu'à la terrasse sur le toit, la boutique du musée est réputée comme un véritable trésor. Le week-end, les DJ chauffent la salle et des spécialités culinaires de groupes ethniques divers sont offertes.

Todo el complejo de este centro de arte en el Queens, antiguamente colegio de niños, está decorado por obras de arte, desde el jardín hasta el mirador del techo, y la tienda es considerada una verdadera caja de tesoros. En los fines de semana la escena se anima con DJs y especialidades culinarias de las distintas culturas.

L'intero complesso di questo centro d'arte del Queens, già scuola elementare, è corredato di opere d'arte dal giardino alla terrazza sul tetto, e il suo negozio è considerato una vera scatola dei tesori. Nel week-end è possibile assistere ad eventi di warm-up con tanto di DJ, e assaggiare le specialità culinarie dei diversi gruppi culturali.

Restaurants Cafés Bars Clubs

In this internationally unique gastronomy scene, you can find every trend and every cuisine of the world. Especially Manhattan is like a culinary fusion workshop. Eat Peruvian food? East African? Kosher? The only problem here may be the reservation. All of the gastronomic price ranges are represented. A generous tip–twice the amount of the bill's tax–is obligatory.

Dans ce milieu gastronomique unique au monde, on trouve chaque tendance et n'importe quelle cuisine du monde. Surtout Manhattan ressemble à un atelier de fusion culinaire. Manger péruvien, est africain, casher ? Pas de problème, sauf peut-être pour la réservation. Toutes les classes de prix sont représentées. Des pourboires généreux – le double des taxes sur l'addition – sont obligatoires.

En esta única escena gastronómica internacional encontramos todas las tendencias y platos del mundo. Manhattan es la que mejor representa esta fusión culinaria: ¿Comida peruana? ¿De África oriental? ¿Kasher? Ningún problema, lo único es reservar por adelantado. Todos los niveles económicos quedan representados y una propina abundante –incluso redoblando la– es obligatoria.

In questa scena gastronomica unica al mondo si trovano tutte le tendenze e le tradizioni culinarie possibili. In particolare Manhattan è una vera e propria centrale di fusione. Ristoranti peruviani? Cucina Est-Africana? Kasher? Nessun problema, basta prenotare. Ce n'è per tutti i gusti e per tutte le tasche. Obbligatoria è una mancia abbondante, addirittura tale da raddoppiare il conto stesso.

Left page: Peasant
Right page: Left EN Japanese Brasserie, right Chinatown

Left page: Top left East Village, top right Meat-packing District, bottom Katz's Delicatessen
Right page: Top Chinatown, bottom East Village

241 Church Street
New York, NY 10013
TriBeCa
Phone: +1 / 212 / 9 25 02 02
www.jean-georges.com

Opening hours: Mon–Wed 5.30 pm to 11 pm, Thu–Sat to midnight, Sun to 10.30 pm
Prices: Entree lunch $ 33, dinner $ 60
Cuisine: Chinese
Public transportation: 1 Franklin Street; A, C Chambers Street
Map: No. 1
Editor's tip: Early reservations recommended! On weekends it can be fully booked a month ahead.

Richard Meier created a friendly, Asian-flavored oasis close to Chinatown: white empty wall areas and indirect lighting radiate tranquility, just the red cloths with Chinese characters set colorful accents. Celebrity chef Jean-Georges Vongerichten and his team conjure up exquisite, Chinese-inspired dishes.

Une oasis d'une allure asiatique près de China-town, crée par Richard Meier. Les murs vides et blancs ainsi que l'éclairage indirect rayonnent le calme, seulement les tissus rouges avec des calligraphies chinoises mettent des accents de couleur. Le cuisinier – « Star » Jean-Georges Vongerichten – et son équipe préparent des repas magiques et raffinés d'inspiration chinoise.

Oasis acogedor de sabor asiático cerca de Chinatown, obra de Richard Meier. Las blancas paredes desnudas y la iluminación indirecta irradian paz, mientras telas rojas con inscripciones chinas dan los únicos toques de color. El célebre chef Jean-Georges Vongerichten y su equipo ofrecen platos exquisitos de inspiración china.

La creazione di Richard Meier è un'accogliente oasi dal sapore asiatico a due passi da China-town. Bianche pareti spoglie e una illuminazione indiretta irradiano tranquillità, mentre drappi rossi con iscrizioni cinesi costituiscono l'unico elemento di colore. Il celebre chef Jean-Georges Vongerichten e il suo team stupiscono con squisiti piatti di ispirazione cinese.

Peasant

194 Elizabeth Street
New York, NY 10012
SoHo
Phone: +1 / 212 / 9 65 95 11
www.peasantnyc.com

Opening hours: Tue–Sun 6 pm to 11 pm, Mon closed
Prices: Menu $ 45
Cuisine: Italian
Public transportation: N, R, W 6 Spring Street; 6 Prince Street
Map: No. 42

This Italian cuisine in SoHo is reliable, respectable, and has the entire palette: mozzarella and prosciutto, pasta and pizza, risotto and gnocchi. The rustic furnishings with their earthy details are reminiscent of an Italian country inn and the food is still cooked over an open flame. The wines come mainly from the southern region of Italy.

De la cuisine italienne dans le SoHo, fiable, solide et avec toute la palette : mozzarella et prosciutto, pâtes et pizza, rizotto et gnocchi. L'intérieur rustique avec des détails traditionnels rappelle un gîte de campagne italienne ; on cuisine encore sur le feu ouvert. Les vins proviennent essentiellement des régions du sud de l'Italie.

Comida italiana en el SoHo, de confianza y sustancia, dotada de la oferta completa: mozzarella y jamón, pasta y pizza, risotto y gnocchi. Los muebles rústicos y los detalles genuinos saben mesón de la campiña italiana, y la comida se cocina todavía a fuego libre. Los vinos proceden en su mayoría de las comarcas del sur de Italia.

Cucina italiana a SoHo, di sostanza e affidabile, e che offre la gamma completa: mozzarella e prosciutto, pasta e pizza, risotto e gnocchi. L'arredamento rustico con dettagli genuini ricorda una trattoria italiana di campagna, e il cibo si cucina ancora a fuoco vivo. I vini provengono prevalentemente dalle regioni meridionali italiane.

Balthazar

80 Spring Street
New York, NY 10012
SoHo
Phone: +1 / 212 / 9 65 17 85
www.balthazarny.com

Opening hours: Mon–Fri 7.30 am to midnight, Sat–Sun 8 am to 1 am
Prices: Menu $ 40–50
Cuisine: French
Public transportation: R, W Prince Street; 6 Spring Street; B, D, F, V Broadway-Lafayette Street
Map: No. 4

In the brasserie that claims it is the best on this side of the Atlantic, you will be seated on coffeehouse furniture upholstered with red leather. Home-baked baguettes are served with oysters, shrimp, steak, and chicken dishes. More than 300 French wines inspire a pleasurable agony of indecision. The desserts are just as seductive.

Dans cette brasserie, qui se veut la meilleure au-delà de l'Atlantique, on est assis sur des meubles de café couverts de cuir rouge. Avec des huîtres, crevettes, steaks et plats au poulet, on sert des baguettes faites maison. Plus de 300 vins français vous mettent dans l'embarras du choix. Les desserts sont également séduisants.

En el café-restaurante que afirma ser el mejor de este lado del Atlántico, encontramos muebles de estilo café francés tapizados en piel roja. Los platos a base de ostras, gambas, bistec y pollo son acompañados por pan blanco casero. Más de 300 vinos franceses provocan el placentero problema de elegir ... y los postres son igualmente seductores.

Nel pub che si vanta di essere la migliore su questo lato dell'Atlantico, l'ospite trova posto su un arredamento in stile coffee house rivestito in cuoio rosso. I piatti a base di ostriche, gamberetti, pollo e bistecche sono accompagnati da pane fatto in casa. Tra gli oltre 300 vini francesi, non c'è che un piacevole imbarazzo della scelta, e i dessert sono altrettanto tentatori.

Katz's Delicatessen

205 East Houston Street
New York, NY 10002
Lower East Side
Phone: +1 / 212 / 2 54 22 46
www.katzdeli.com

Opening hours: Sun+Tue 8 am to 10 pm, Wed+Thu to 11 pm, Fri+Sat to 3 am
Prices: Soups, burgers $ 5, sandwiches $ 13, grill platter $ 20, Katz's salami $ 10
Cuisine: Traditional New Yorker style
Public transportation: F, J, M, Z Delancey Street-Essex Street; V 2 Avenue-Lower East Side
Map: No. 27
Editor's tip: The salami and pastrami sandwiches are legendary.

The legendary deli on the Lower East Side has existed since 1888 and even made it to the silver screen: Harry and Sally had their famous date here. The shop still entices some celebrities. There are salads, soups, burgers, barbecue dishes, and supposedly the best sandwiches in New York.

Ce deli sur le Lower East Side existe depuis 1888 et a fait son chemin jusqu'au cinéma : c'est ici que Harry et Sally ont eu leur rendez-vous célèbre. Le magasin attire souvent des célébrités. Dans une atmosphère légère, on sert des salades, soupes, burgers grillades et soi-disant les meilleurs sandwichs de New York.

El legendario deli en la Lower East Side, en 1888 ha llegado hasta al cine: aquí Harry y Sally tuvieron su famosa cita, y algunos famosos se dejan atrapar por él. Bajo una atmósfera informal encontramos ensaladas, sopas, hamburguesas, parrilladas y, al parecer, los mejores sándwich de Nueva York.

Il leggendario deli sulla Lower East Side esiste dal 1888, ed è arrivato fin sullo schermo: è qui che Harry e Sally hanno avuto il loro famoso appuntamento, e non è raro trovare qui qualche celebrità. In un'atmosfera informale si gustano insalate, minestre, hamburger, piatti alla griglia e (a quanto pare) i migliori sandwich di New York.

Kittichai

60 Thompson Street
New York, NY 10014
SoHo
Phone: +1 / 212 / 2 19 20 00
www.kittichairestaurant.com

Opening hours: Mon–Fri noon to 2.45 pm, Sat+Sun 11 am to 2.45 pm, Sun–Wed 5.30 pm to 11 pm, Thu–Sat 5.30 pm to midnight
Prices: Entree $ 25
Cuisine: Thai
Public transportation: C, E Spring Street
Map: No. 29

The SoHo restaurant that has won many awards offers the best Thai food in the United States. A clear design, soft light, and Far Eastern elements of décor form the framework for the classy cuisine: salads with broiled slices of beef, chicken breast in bright-yellow curry sauce, coconut crêpes, and creative cocktails.

Ce restaurant dans le SoHo, qui a gagné plusieurs prix, offre la meilleure cuisine, « Thai » aux Etats-Unis. Un design clair, lumière douce et décoration d'Extrême-Orient créent le cadre pour la noble cuisine : des salades avec des tranches de bœuf, poitrine de poulet avec sauce curry fort jaune, crêpes à la noix de coco et des cocktails créatifs.

Este restaurante del SoHo, varias veces premiado, presenta la mejor comida tailandesa de los Estados Unidos. Un diseño despejado, luz suave y una decoración de sabor asiático forman la escena alrededor de la noble cocina: ensaladas con filetes de buey a la parrilla, pechugas de pollo en salsa curry amarillo brillante, crêpes de coco y creativos cócteles.

Questo pluri-premiato ristorante di SoHo offre la migliore cucina thai negli Stati Uniti. Un design chiaro, luci soffuse ed elementi decorativi dal sapore asiatico fanno da contorno ideale alla nobile cucina: insalate con fettine di manzo ai ferri, petti di pollo in salsa al curry giallo vivo, crêpes di noci di cocco e cocktail creativi.

EN Japanese Brasserie

435 Hudson Street
New York, NY 10014
West Village
Phone: +1 / 212 / 6 47 91 96
www.enjb.com

Opening hours: Sun–Thu 5.30 pm to 11 pm, Fri+Sat 5.30 pm to midnight
Prices: Menu $ 60
Cuisine: Japanese
Public transportation: 1, 9 Houston Street; A, B, C, D, E, F, V West 4 Street
Map: No. 17

Exquisite fish, exotic vegetables, and tasty rice are served here. The well-stocked bar offers Yamagata sake, which is only made in the northwest of Japan and served just here in New York. It is fruitier than the customary sake. The especially pure Yamagata water is also available here.

Ici on sert des poissons exquis, légumes exotiques et du ris délicieux. Dans le bar, bien équipé, on offre du saké Yamagata, qui est produit uniquement dans le nord-ouest du Japon et servi uniquement ici à New york. Il est plus fruité que le saké ordinaire. Ici, on trouve aussi l'eau Yamagata qui et spécialement pure.

Aquí se sirven distinguidos pescados, verduras exóticas y un exquisito arroz. El bar es muy bien surtido y ofrece sake Yamagata, producido exclusivamente en el noroeste de Japón y servido solo aquí en Nueva York, más afrutado que el sake tradicional. También se puede además encontrar el agua Yamagata, de pureza excepcional.

Qui si servono pesce pregiato, verdure esotiche e riso prelibato. Il bar ben fornito offre sakè Yamagata, distillato esclusivamente nel Giappone nord-occidentale e servito solo qui a New York, dal sapore più fruttato rispetto al sakè tradizionale. Si può trovare inoltre l'eccezionalmente pura acqua Yamagata.

The Mercer Kitchen

99 Prince Street
New York, NY 10012
SoHo
Phone: +1 / 212 / 9 66 54 54
www.jean-georges.com

Opening hours: Daily 8 am to 11 am, noon to 3 pm and 6 pm to midnight
Prices: Entree $ 25
Cuisine: Modern American
Public transportation: R, W Prince Street; 6 Spring Street
Map: No. 34

In the truest sense of the word, this kitchen is concealed in the elegant hotel of the same name: The restaurant is located on the lower level, hidden beneath the sidewalks of SoHo. The furnishings by Christian Liaigre are modern-rustic and the lighting is warm and discrete. You can watch the chefs perform their art in the open-design kitchen.

Cette cuisine se cache dans l'hôtel élégant du même nom – au vrai sens du mot : le restaurant se trouve au sous-sol, caché sous les trottoirs de SoHo. L'intérieur de Christian Liaigre est moderne-rustique. L'éclairage chaud et discret. Dans la cuisine ouverte, vous pouvez observer les cuisiniers dans l'exercice de leur art.

La cocina está soterrada en el elegante hotel de mismo nombre ... literalmente: el restaurante está en el subsuelo, oculto bajo las aceras del SoHo. La decoración de Christian Liaigre es de estilo moderno-rústico y la luz es suave y discreta. A través de su cocina abierta, es posible observar a los cocineros en todo su arte.

Una cucina sepolta nell'omonimo elegante hotel ... nel vero senso della parola: il ristorante si trova in un sotterraneo, nascosto sotto i marciapiedi di SoHo. L'arredamento di Christian Liaigre è in stile moderno-rustico e le luci sono calde e discrete. È possibile osservare i cuochi all'opera attraverso la cucina a struttura aperta.

Spice Market

403 West 13th Street
New York, NY 10014
Meatpacking District
Phone: +1 / 212 / 6 75 23 22
www.jean-georges.com

Opening hours: Mon–Fri noon to 4 pm, Mon–Sun 5.30 pm to midnight, brunch Sat+Sun noon to 4 pm
Prices: Entree lunch $ 40, dinner $ 50
Cuisine: Southeast Asian
Public transportation: A, C, E, L 14 Street-Eighth Avenue; 1 14 Street
Map: No. 46

You can immediately feel the passion for the East-Asian flair and bazaars here. The furnishings of this hot spot in the Meatpacking District are original oriental, the lighting is subdued, and the rooms are kept in gentle colors. Jean-Georges Vongerichten and his team will pamper you with sophisticated, exotic dishes.

Ici, on sent tout de suite la passion pour le flair-asiatique et pour les bazars. L'intérieur de ce point chaud dans le Meatpacking District est original oriental, l'éclairage décent et les salles sont tenues en couleurs douces. Jean-Georges Vongerichten et son équipe vous gâtent avec des repas exotiques raffinés.

Aquí nos dejamos inmediatamente transportar hacia los perfumes asiáticos y los bazares. La decoración de este punto de atracción del Distrito de los Carniceros es originalmente asiática, el local posee una iluminación discreta y las salas presentan colores suaves. Jean-Georges Vongerichten y su equipo nos miman con sus exquisitos platos exóticos.

Qui ci si lascia trasportare immediatamente ai profumi dell'Estremo Oriente e ai bazar. L'arredamento di questo "punto caldo" nel Meatpacking District è originale asiatico, l'illuminazione è discreta e le sale presentano colori tenui. Jean-Georges Vongerichten e il suo team vi viziano con pietanze esotiche e sofisticate.

Matsuri

369 West 16th Street
New York, NY 10011
Chelsea
Phone: +1 / 212 / 2 43 64 00
www.themaritimehotel.com/
matsuri.html

Opening hours: Sun–Wed 6 pm to 1.30 am, Thu–Sat 6 pm to
2.30 am
Prices: Entree $ 20, drinks $ 14
Cuisine: Japanese
Public transportation: A, C, E 14 Street-Eighth Avenue
Map: No. 33

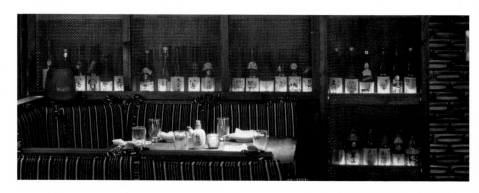

Many of the locals consider the restaurant in the "Maritime Hotel" to be one of the best Japanese eateries in New York. In addition to sushi, you can order all of the classic fish dishes from Japan and watch as your meal is prepared directly in front of your eyes. The delicacies are served with the finest rice and choice types of vegetables. More than 200 types of sake are on the menu.

Pour de nombreux habitants locaux, le restaurant dans le « Maritime Hotel » est un des meilleurs restaurants Japonais à New York. A côté de Sushi, on sert ici tous les repas de poissons classiques du Japon, qui sont préparés directement devant vos yeux. Les délicatesses sont servies avec du ris très fin et des légumes sélectionnés. Il y a plus de 200 sortes de saké disponibles.

Para muchos nativos el restaurante del "Maritime Hotel" es uno de los mejores japoneses de Nueva York. Además de sushi, hay típicas especialidades de pescado japonesas, preparadas delante de nuestros ojos. Las exquisiteces son acompañadas por fino arroz y verduras seleccionadas. La carta incluye más de 200 variedades de sake.

Parecchi indigeni considerano il ristorante del "Maritime Hotel" come uno dei migliori locali giapponesi di New York. Oltre al sushi vi si gustano tutti i piatti di pesce tipici giapponesi, preparati direttamente davanti ai vostri occhi. Le squisitezze sono accompagnate da riso sopraffino e verdure scelte. L'offerta comprende oltre 200 tipi di sakè.

Dévi

8 East 18th Street
New York, NY 10003
Flatiron
Phone: +1 / 212 / 6 91 13 00
www.devinyc.com

Opening hours: Mon–Thu noon to 2.30 pm, 5.30 pm to
10.30 pm, Fri+Sat noon to 2.30 pm, 5.30 pm to 11 pm, Sun 5 pm
to 10 pm
Prices: Appetizers from $ 6, entrees from $ 14
Cuisine: Indian
Public transportation: 4, 5, 6, L, N, Q, R, W 14 Street-Union Square
Map: No. 15

Suvir Saran and Hemant Mathur offer authentic Indian cuisine. Saran has become one of the respected authorities in the USA and Mathur is among the ten top tandoori masters. They use organically grown, fresh products and spice them exquisitely. Warm tones and tastefully designed Indian décor set the mood for the interior.

Suvir Saran et Hemant Mathur offrent de la cuisine indienne authentique. En cela, Saran est une autorité reconnue aux USA et Mathur est parmi les premiers maîtres du Tandoori. Ils utilisent des produits frais d'agriculture écologique et offrent un assaisonnement exquis. L'intérieur est marqué par des couleurs chaudes et une décoration indienne de très bon goût.

Suvir Saran y Hemant Mathur ofrecen una auténtica comida india. Saran es considerado en Estados Unidos una autoridad en esta materia, y Mathur es uno de los diez maestros de Tandoori. Los productos son frescos, ecológicos y exquisitamente especiados. Tonos cálidos y una decoración india de buen gusto caracterizan el interior.

Suvir Saran e Hemant Mathur offrono autentica cucina indiana. Saran è riconosciuto come un'autorità in questa materia in tutti gli Stati Uniti, e Mathur è ritenuto tra i primi dieci maestri di tandoori. Si impiegano prodotti freschi e di coltivazione biologica, squisitamente speziati. Toni caldi e decorazioni indiane di buon gusto caratterizzano l'ambiente.

Keens Steakhouse

72 West 36th Street
New York, NY 10018
Midtown
Phone: +1 / 212 / 9 47 36 36
www.keens.com

Opening hours: Mon–Fri 11.45 am to 10.30 pm, Sat 5 pm to 10.30 pm, Sun 5 pm to 9 pm
Prices: Entree $ 40
Cuisine: American
Public transportation: B, D, F, N, Q, R, V, W 34 Street-Herald Square
Map: No. 28

The restaurant, which opened in 1885, upholds the tradition of pipe-smoking with about 50,000 historical pipes decorating the ceiling. The meals also have a tradition: for example, the legendary leg of mutton or the turkey that soaks in dark beer for three days. These are served with home-brewed beer and home-baked bread.

La maison, établie en 1885, célèbre la tradition de fumer la pipe ; le plafond est orné d'environ 50 000 pipes historiques. Les repas aussi ont de la tradition : par exemple le légendaire gigot de mouton ou le dindonneau qui a passé trois jours dans de la bière brune. On sert également des bières et des pains faits maison.

Abierto en 1885, mantiene la tradición de fumar en pipa, con sus más de 50 000 pipas históricas colgando del techo. Los platos también tienen tradición: como el legendario muslo de carnero, o el pavo macerado tres días en cerveza negra. Todo acompañado con cerveza y pan caseros.

Questo locale, aperto nel 1885, tiene alta la tradizione del fumo della pipa, con circa 50 000 pipe storiche che adornano il soffitto. Anche le pietanze hanno tradizione: come il leggendaro cosciotto di montone, o il tacchino marinato per tre giorni in birra scura. Il tutto servito con birra di produzione propria e pane fatto in casa.

Shopping

New York—the ultimate shopping experience. An enormous range of merchandise is available, and the favorable exchange rate for the dollar also makes it attractive to travelers. The major brands are sold on Fifth Avenue, as well as Madison Avenue, and parts of Broadway with its side streets. You can find bargains at the sales or in the superstores. Tip: the well-known designer wear costs somewhat less at department stores than in the boutiques.

New York – l'ultime expérience pour les course. Le choix de marchandises est énorme et le taux du dollar avantageux fait le reste. Sur la Cinquième Avenue, on trouve toutes les grandes marques ainsi qu'à Madison Avenue, certains endroits de Broadway avec ses rues latérales. Des bonnes affaires sont disponibles aux soldes ou dans les super-stores. Un conseil : dans les grands magasins, on offre des produits de marque moins chers que dans les boutiques.

Nueva York: el shopping extremo. La oferta es inmensa, favorecida aún más por ser en dólares. En la Quinta Avenida, se encuentran las marcas más famosas, y lo mismo en la Avenida Madison, en Broadway y en sus calles laterales. Las mejores compras se hacen en rebajas y en los superstores, y los grandes almacenes ofrecen prendas de firmas famosas a precios más económico que en las boutiques.

New York: lo shopping estremo. L'offerta è immensa, e per di più il cambio favorevole del dollaro dà una mano. Sulla Fifth Avenue si trovano le firme più prestigiose, così come in Madison Avenue, in parte di Broadway e delle sue vie laterali. I migliori affari si fanno nelle svendite o nei super-store. Un consiglio: nei grandi magazzini si trovano capi firmati a prezzi più convenienti che nelle boutique.

Left page: Fifth Avenue
Right page: Left East Village, right Apple Store Fifth Avenue

Left page: Top left Sotheby's, right SoHo, bottom Chinatown
Right page: Top SoHo, bottom Tiffany & Co. on Fifth Avenue

TIFFANY & CO.

Century 21 Department Stores

22 Cortlandt Street
New York, NY 10007
Financial District
Phone: +1 / 212 / 2 27 90 92
www.c21stores.com

Opening hours: Mon–Fri 7.45 am to 8 pm, Sat 10 am to 8 pm,
Sun 11 am to 7 pm
Products: Discount market for clothing, shoes, cosmetics, home
accessories
Public transportation: R, W Cortlandt Street; R, W Rector Street
Map: No. 11
Editor's tip: Make a day of it as it takes time to rummage through
the cramped shelves and the tables bursting with goods.

Directly across from Ground Zero, the three floors of Century 21 offer everything that usually just the stars and the rich can afford and at inexpensive prices reduced up to 75 %. The shopper can find designer pieces by Versace or Prada, as well as bargains in cosmetic products, home accessories, and household appliances.

Directement en face de Ground Zero, Century 21 offre sur trois étages tous les articles qui, d'habitude, ne sont portés que par les vedettes et les riches et ceci avec des réductions jusqu'à 75 %. Ainsi, on y trouve des articles design de Versace ou Prada et des bonnes affaires parmi les produits cosmétiques, les accessoires de maison et articles ménagers.

Ubicado frente a la Zona Cero, ofrece en sus tres plantas aquello que suele ser exclusivamente de ricos y famosos, pero con descuentos de hasta un 75 %. Se pueden encontrar prendas de Alta Costura firmadas por Versace y Prada, y productos cosméticos y para el hogar a precios muy atractivos.

Situato direttamente di fronte a Ground Zero, Century 21 offre su tre piani ciò che abitualmente è riservato ai ricchi e famosi ... con il vantaggio di sconti fino al 75 %. Si possono trovare capi d'alta moda firmati Versace o Prada, così come cosmetici, casalinghi e accessori per la casa a prezzi d'affare.

Dean & DeLuca

560 Broadway
New York, NY 10012
SoHo
Phone: +1 / 212 / 2 26 68 00
www.deandeluca.com

Opening hours: Mon–Fri 7 am to 9 pm, Sat 8 am to 9 pm, Sun 8 am to 8 pm
Products: Chocolates, pastries, delicatessen, convenience foods, accessories
Public transportation: N, R, W Prince Street; B, D, F, V Broadway-Lafayette Street; 6 Bleeker Street
Map: No. 14

Only the finest delicacies from around the world are found here, including cheese and ham, pasta and antipasti, spices and pastries. Kitchenware from the famous design studios, cookbooks, fine wine, and glassware complete the luxuriant offer of fragrant treats. The espresso bar serves homemade cakes, which are ideal for a shopping break.

Ici, on ne trouve que les plus nobles délicatesses du monde entier, y compris du fromage, jambon, des pâtes et antipasti, épices et pâtisseries. Des articles de cuisine des studios de design connus, livres de cuisine, des vins excellents et des articles en verre complètent l'offre abondante des gourmandises délicieuses. Au bar-expresso, on trouve des gâteaux faits maison, idéals pour une pause « shopping ».

Aquí sólo se encuentran los manjares más exquisitos de cualquier parte del mundo, incluidos quesos y jamones, pasta y entrantes, especias y tartas. Trastos de cocina de los más famosos estudios de diseño, libros de cocina, preciados vinos y buena cristalería completan la magnífica oferta. Los dulces caseros en el bar son ideales para hacer una pausa entre las compras.

Qui si trovano solamente le delicatezze più raffinate da tutto il mondo, tra cui formaggi e prosciutti, pasta e antipasti, spezie e biscotti. Oggetti da cucina dei più famosi studi di design, libri di cucina, vini pregiati e cristalleria completano la sontuosa offerta di profumate ghiottonerie. I dolci fatti in casa del bar-espresso sono ideali per una pausa nello shopping.

Strand Book Store

828 Broadway
New York, NY 10003
Greenwich Village
Phone: +1 / 212 / 4 73 14 52
www.strandbooks.com

Opening hours: Mon–Sat 9.30 am to 10.30 pm, Sun 11 am to 10.30 pm
Products: Books
Public transportation: 4, 5, 6, L, N, Q, R, W 14 Street-Union Square
Map: No. 49

This traditional bookstore has five floors that hold almost 19 miles of books, including very special and unusual titles such as first and signed book editions, rare photography books, and collector's items. Its special offers are popular—with discounts up to 50 %, even on new publications.

Dans cette librairie traditionnelle, vous trouvez presque 30 km de livres sur cinq étages, y compris des titres spéciaux et extraordinaires comme des premières éditions et editions signés, des livres de photographies rares et des offres spéciales – jusqu'à 50 % de réduction sont accordés, même sur les nouvelles éditions.

En esta histórica librería encontramos a lo largo de sus cinco plantas casi 30 km de libros, entre ellos títulos especiales y poco comunes como primeras ediciones o copias firmadas, libros fotográficos raros y piezas de coleccionista. Muy apreciadas son sus ofertas especiales, con descuentos de hasta el 50 %, incluso en últimas ediciones.

In questa storica libreria si trovano su cinque piani quasi 30 km di libri, inclusi titoli assai speciali e poco comuni come prime edizioni e copie firmate, rari libri fotografici e pezzi da collezione. Molto popolari sono le offerte speciali, con sconti fino al 50 % anche su edizioni recenti.

MoMA Design and Book Store

11 West 53 Street
New York, NY 10019
Midtown
Phone: +1 / 212 / 7 08 97 00
www.momastore.org

Opening hours: Sat–Thu 9.30 am to 6.30 pm, Fri to 9 pm
Products: Art books, posters, postcards, design, gifts
Public transportation: E, V 5 Avenue; B, D, F, V 47–50 Streets-
Rockefeller Center
Map: No. 36

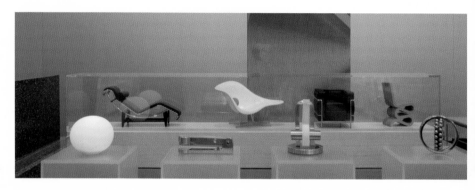

This museum shop is a true sensation: in addition to everything for the art lover, it also offers décor and everyday items from the museum's warehouses for which there is no longer a use. This includes Picasso art prints or modern Chinese flower vases. The book department also has an outstanding assortment.

Cette boutique de musée est une véritable sensation : elle n'offre pas seulement tout pour l'amateur d'art mais aussi des décors et articles courants en provenance des dépôts du musée, qui ne sont plus utilisés. Ceci comprend des reproductions de Picasso ou des vases chinois modernes. La section des livres aussi est trè bien organisée.

Esta tienda del museo es una auténtica sensación: ofrece todo lo imaginable a los aficionados al arte, además de sus decoraciones y objetos de uso cotidiano procedentes de los almacenes del museo, incluso grabados de Picasso y vasos chinos de arte moderno. Magníficamente provista está su sección de libros.

Questo negozio-museo è un'autentica sensazione: non solo offre tutto per gli appassionati d'arte, ma anche decorazioni e oggetti d'uso quotidiano provenienti dai magazzini del museo e che non vengono più impiegati, comprese stampe artistiche di Picasso e vasi cinesi moderni. E anche la sezione libri ha un'assortimento eccezionale.

Rizzoli Bookstore

31 West 57th Street
New York, NY 10019
Midtown
Phone: +1 / 212 / 7 59 24 24
www.rizzoliusa.com

Opening hours: Mon–Fri 10 am to 7.30 pm, Sat 11 am to 7.30 pm, Sun 11 am to 7 pm
Products: Books on art history, architecture, photography, fashion, design and travel, children's books, calendars and CDs
Public transportation: F 57 Street; N, R, W Fifth Avenue-59 Street
Map: No. 44

This is a temple for all types of printed material, gifts, and graphic design. Rizzoli is an institution with utmost prestige. People wear reading glasses on chains around their necks here, curiously approach the big tables full of bestsellers, and pace up and down the rows of shelves. The enormous range is highlighted by chandeliers.

Un temple pour l'imprimé de tout genre, des cadeaux et le design graphique. Rizzoli est une institution de prestige. Ici, les gens portent des lunettes de lecture avec chaîne autour du cou, s'approchent attentivement des grandes tables couvertes de best sellers et défilent devant les rayons. L'énorme offre est mise en scène par les lustres.

Un templo de la palabra estampada, desde regalos hasta diseño gráfico, Rizzoli es una institución de prestigio absoluto. Los clientes pasean con sus gafas para leer colgando de cadenitas al cuello, se acercan con expectación a las mesas llenas de superventas y recorren sus estanterías. La fabulosa oferta es enmarcada por la luz de candelabros.

Un tempio del materiale stampato di ogni tipo, dal regalo al disegno grafico, Rizzoli è un'istituzione del massimo prestigio. Qui è tipico vedere i clienti con gli occhiali che pendono da catenine al collo, che si avvicinano speranzosi ai grossi tavoli pieni di bestseller e girano tra gli scaffali. La scena sull'enorme offerta è completata dalla luce dei candelieri.

Apple Store Fifth Avenue

767 Fifth Avenue
New York, NY 10153
Midtown
Phone: +1 / 212 / 3 36 14 40
www.apple.com/retail/
fifthavenue

Opening hours: Daily 24 hours
Products: Macintosh hardware, iPods, Mac accessories
Public transportation: N, R, W Fifth Avenue-59 Street; F 57 Street;
4, 5, 6 59 Street
Map: No. 3

A glass cube between the skyscrapers on Fifth Avenue serves as an eyecatcher and entrance to the newly opened Apple Flagship Store. This is where the curious can test software and games on fast laptops and computers, as well as the latest iPods and iPhones. Almost 300 experts advise and provide tips.

Un cube en verre entre les gratte-ciels de la Cinquième Avenue sert d'attraction et d'entrée à ce magasin Apple-Flagship-Store qui vient d'ouvrir. Ici, les curieux testent des logiciels et des jeux sur les ordinateurs et des portables rapides ainsi que les nouveaux iPods et iPhones. Presque 300 assistants donnent des conseils.

Un cubo de cristal entre los rascacielos de la Quinta Avenida sirve de reclamo y de entrada a la tienda Apple-Flagship, recientemente abierta. Aquí, los curiosos pueden probar software y juegos en rápidos ordenadores portátiles y de sobremesa y también los más nuevos iPods e iPhones, asesorados por casi 300 expertos.

Un cubo di vetro tra i grattacieli della Fifth Avenue funge da richiamo e da ingresso per il recentemente riaperto Apple-Flagship-Store. Qui i curiosi possono testare software e giochi su veloci computer portatili e PC, oltre ai nuovi iPod e iPhone, assistiti e consigliati da quasi 300 specialisti.

FAO Schwarz

767 Fifth Avenue
New York, NY 10153
Midtown
Phone: +1 / 212 / 6 44 94 00
www.fao.com

Opening hours: Mon–Sat 10 am to 7 pm, Sun 11 am to 6 pm
Products: Toys
Public transportation: N, R, W Fifth Avenue-59 Street;
F 57 Street; 4, 5, 6 59 Street
Map: No. 18

This store, opened by the German immigrant Frederick August Otto Schwarz in 1870, has fulfilled children's dreams for generations—even the more demanding ones: it has absolutely everything from the classic Steiff stuffed animal to a motorized Mini-Cooper. Even a Victorian children's villa for the yard at home is available for $ 22,000.

Ce magasin, ouvert en 1870 par l'immigrant allemand Frederick August Otto Schwarz, réalise des rêves d'enfant, même les plus exigeants, depuis des générations : ici, on trouve tout, de l'animal en peluche Steiff jusqu'au mini cooper motorisé. Même une petite villa ou la maison pour $ 22 000.

Esta tienda, abierta por el inmigrante alemán Frederick August Otto Schwarz en 1870, ha cumplido durante generaciones los deseos de los niños, hasta los más atrevidos: hay de todo, desde los clásicos peluches de Steiff hasta un Mini-Cooper motorizado, e incluso una casita de niños victoriana valorada en 22 000 $.

Da diverse generazioni questo negozio, aperto dall'immigrante tedesco Frederick August Otto Schwarz nel 1870, esaudisce i desideri dei bambini, anche i più esigenti: vi si trova davvero di tutto, dai classici peluche Steiff alle Mini Cooper a motore, e persino una villa vittoriana in miniatura da 22 000 $ per il giardino.

For Your Convenience

FAO Schwarz will ship
your purchase
anywhere in the world.

Shipping provided by FedEx on the Lower Level

Hotels

September 11, 2001 hit Manhattan's hotel industry especially hard. Yet, after hoteliers modernized their buildings at an enormous expense, visitors are now streaming back into the city and the scene is as varied as never before: from the luxury hotels to the design category and reputable middle-class establishments to the comfortable bed & breakfasts and apartments—everything is represented here, even in terms of price.

Le 11 septembre 2001 a gravement touché l'hôtellerie de Manhattan. Cependant, les hôteliers ont modernisé leurs bâtiments avec des efforts énormes, les visiteurs reviennent dans la ville et la scène est plus vivante que jamais : des hôtels de luxe aux maisons de design, et de classe moyenne jusqu' aux confortables « Bed and Breakfast » et appartements, tout est possible – même au niveau du prix.

El 11 Septiembre de 2001 llevó a Manhattan a un momento duro, pero tras los enormes esfuerzos que muchos propietarios realizaron por renovar sus establecimientos, la ciudad se llena una vez más de visitantes y la escena es tán heterogénea o más que antes. Desde hoteles de lujo o prácticos hoteles de media categoría y de diseño hasta confortables bed & breakfast y apartamentos, todo es representado, y para todas las economías.

L'11 settembre 2001 portò a un periodo piuttosto duro per l'industria alberghiera di Manhattan, eppure dopo che molti albergatori hanno modernizzato gli impianti con sforzi enormi, i visitatori hanno ripreso ad affluire e la scena è più variopinta che mai. Dai Grand Hotel a pratici alberghi di media categoria e design fino a confortevoli bed & breakfast e appartamenti ce n'è davvero per tutti, anche nei prezzi.

Left page: Plaza Athénée
Right page: Left Hotel (The Mercer), right Four Seasons Hotel

Hotel on Rivington

107 Rivington Street
New York, NY 10002
Lower East Side
Phone: +1 / 212 / 4 75 26 00
Fax: +1 / 212 / 4 75 59 59
www.hotelonrivington.com

Prices: Double room, suite from $ 325 to $ 5 000
Public transportation: F Delancey Street; J, M, Z Essex Street
Map: No. 25

The hotel in the 21-floor glass tower on the Lower East Side offers an unbelievable view of New York from every vantage point. Renowned international designers have contributed their talents to this contemporary hotel. The "Thor" restaurant and the fashion and design shop "Annie O" are among the top addresses of this hip quarter.

Cet hôtel dans la tour vitrée de 21 étages sur le Lower East Side offre une vue spectaculaire sur New York de chaque point de vue. Des designers de renom international ont participé à la conception de cet hôtel contemporain. Le restaurant « Thor » et la boutique de design et de mode « Annie O » comptent parmi les meilleures adresses de ce quartier branché.

El hotel se encuentra en una torre de cristal de 21 pisos en la Lower East Side, y ofrece desde todos los puntos una vista maravillosa de Nueva York. Diseñadores de renombre internacional han dejado sus marcas en este hotel contemporáneo. El restaurante "Thor" y la tienda de moda y diseño "Annie O" pertenecen a la élite del sector.

L'hotel si trova nella torre di vetro alta 21 piani sulla Lower East Side, e da ogni punto offre una vista fantastica su New York. Rinomati designer internazionali hanno lasciato il loro segno su questo hotel dal carattere contemporaneo. Il ristorante "Thor" e il negozio di moda e design "Annie O" appartengono alla élite della zona.

Hotel (The Mercer)

147 Mercer Street
New York, NY 10012
SoHo
Phone: +1 / 212 / 9 66 60 60
Fax: +1 / 212 / 9 65 38 38
www.mercerhotel.com

Prices: Double room from $ 495, suite from $ 1 350
Services: Packing and unpacking service
Public transportation: 6 Spring Street; N, R, W Prince Street;
B, D, F, V Broadway-Lafayette Street
Map: No. 23

The hotel in SoHo conveys the experience of living in a modern loft with its dignified neo-Romanesque architecture. The 75 elegant rooms, studios, and suites are furnished in a stylish, unobtrusive manner. The restaurant is inviting and informal, with international cuisine and an enormous range of wines.

Cet hôtel dans le SoHo avec sa solide architecture néoromane donne le sentiment d'habiter dans un loft moderne. Les 75 chambres, studios et suites sont élégants, chics et aménagés avec le plus grand soin. Le restaurant est accueillant et décontracté avec une cuisine internationale et un énorme choix de vins.

Este hotel en el SoHo transmite la sensación de vivir en un loft moderno, con una muy bien cuidada arquitectura neorománica. Posee 75 habitaciones, estudios y suites, elegantemente amuebladas sin ser recargadas. El restaurante es acogedor y familiar, con una cocina internacional y una extensa oferta de vinos.

Questo hotel di SoHo trasmette la sensazione di vivere in un moderno loft, con la sua curatissima architettura neoromanica. Comprende 75 tra camere, studi e suite, dall'arredamento elegante e non invadente. Il ristorante è accogliente e informale, con cucina internazionale e un'offerta di vini enorme.

Hotel Gansevoort

18 9th Avenue
New York, NY 10014
Meatpacking District
Phone: +1 / 212 / 2 06 67 00
Fax: +1 / 212 / 2 55 58 58
www.hotelgansevoort.com

Prices: Rooms from $ 435, suites from $ 675
Facilities: Roof garden, swimming pool with underwater music, 360° city view
Public transportation: A, C, E, L 14 Street-Eighth Avenue
Map: No. 24

This luxury hotel with its clear, modern design is situated in the middle of the Meatpacking District—which was once the center of New York's meat industry. The heated swimming pool offers a wonderful view of the Hudson River. The hotel, which bears the official name of the quarter, is also popular with artists.

Au centre du Meatpacking District – un quartier branché, autrefois centre de l'industrie de la viande – se trouve cet hôtel de luxe dans un design clair et moderne. A partir de la piscine chauffée, on a une vue magnifique sur la rivière Hudson. L'hôtel, qui porte le nom officiel du quartier, est également très apprécié par les artistes.

Este hotel de lujo, de diseño moderno y despejado, se encuentra en el centro del Distrito de los Carniceros, antiguo núcleo de la industria de la carne de Nueva York y ahora barrio de "tendencia". Desde la piscina calentada tenemos una magnífica vista del río Hudson. El hotel es conocido por el nombre oficial del barrio, y es muy apreciado por los artistas.

Questo hotel di lusso, dal design chiaro e moderno, si trova in mezzo al Meatpacking District, antico centro dell'industria della carne a New York, e ora quartiere "di tendenza". Dalla piscina riscaldata si gode una gran vista sull'Hudson River. L'hotel prende il nome dalla denominazione ufficiale del quartiere, ed è anche prediletto dagli artisti.

The Maritime Hotel

363 West 16th Street
New York, NY 10011
Chelsea
Phone: +1 / 212 / 2 42 43 00
Fax: +1 / 212 / 2 42 11 88
www.themaritimehotel.com

Prices: Room from $ 315 to $ 425
Public transportation: A, C, E, L 14 Street-Eighth Avenue
Map: No. 32

The building with maritime flair has furnishings that are elegant but not stiff. The rooms have extra-wide beds and the fitness area is open around the clock. "La Bottega" offers Italian country cuisine, "Matsuri" serves cultivated Japanese food, and both bars stock an impressive range of liquor.

La maison avec son flair maritime est ameublée de façon élégante mais pas froide. Les chambres offrent des lits extra-larges et le centre de remise en forme est ouvert en permanence. Dans « La Bottega », on vous offre de la cuisine rustique italienne, le « Matsuri » sert de la cuisine japonaise raffinée et les deux bars ont un répertoire impressionant de spiritueux.

Este edificio con sabor marinero tiene una distinguida elegancia, sin ser demasiado formal ni rígido. En las habitaciones hay camas extra-anchas y la zona fitness está abierta a cualquier hora. El restaurante "La Bottega" ofrece cocina casera italiana, en el "Matsuri" hay comida japonesa muy bien cuidada, mientras que los dos bares ofrecen una asombrosa variedad de licores.

L'edificio di sapore marinaresco possiede una certa eleganza, senza apparire troppo formale. Le camere hanno letti amplissimi e la zona fitness è aperta a tutte le ore. Il ristorante "La Bottega" offre cucina casereccia italiana, "Matsuri" presenta cucina giapponese ben curata, mentre i due bar servono un'impressionante varietà di liquori.

Bryant Park Hotel

40 West 40th Street
New York, NY 10018
Midtown
Phone: +1 / 212 / 8 69 01 00
Fax: +1 / 212 / 8 69 44 46
www.bryantparkhotel.com

Prices: Room from $ 495
Facilities: 112 rooms, 17 suites, Cellar Bar, Japanese restaurant
Public transportation: 1, 2, 3, 7, N, Q, R, S, W 42 Street-Times Square
Map: No. 9

The façade of the trendy art deco hotel turns into a large display window in the entrance area. The interior stands out with its reduced, stylish furnishings. In addition to more than 100 rooms and 20 suites, as well as an exquisite restaurant, it offers a small private movie theater. Bryant Park is directly in front of the door.

La façade de cet hôtel branché Art Déco se transforme, à l'entrée, en une grande vitrine. L'intérieur séduit avec un style réducteur. A côté de plus de 100 chambres et 20 suites, il y a a un restaurant exquis et un petit cinéma privé. Le Bryant Park se trouve directement devant la porte.

La fachada de este célebre hotel art-deco se transforma en un gran escaparate al entrar en la hall. El interior impacta por el reducido mobiliario, con mucho estilo. Además de 100 habitaciones y 20 suites y del exquisito restaurante, ofrece un pequeño cine privado. El Bryant Park está justo frente a la entrada.

La facciata di questo hotel art-déco all'ultimo grido si trasforma in una vetrina all'entrare nella hall. L'interno si fa notare per l'arredamento ridotto e di stile. Oltre a più di 100 camere e 20 suite e allo squisito ristorante dispone anche di un piccolo cinema privato. Il Bryant Park si trova direttamente fuori dalla porta.

Hotel QT

125 West 45th Street
New York, NY 10036
Times Square
Phone: +1 / 212 / 3 54 23 23
Fax: +1 / 212 / 3 02 85 85
www.hotelqt.com

Prices: Double room from $ 200, suite from $ 375
Facilities: Lobby with pool, sauna, kiosk
Public transportation: 1, 2, 3, 7, N, Q, R, S, W 42 Street-Times Square
Map: No. 26

The design hotel by André Balazs makes it possible for you to live with a view of Times Square. With their inventive and practical furnishings, many of the rooms have bunk beds for an optimal use of space. The sauna and steam room provide relaxation. You can socialize in the "Mezzanine Lounge", at the bar, and around the pool.

Cet hôtel design d'André Balazs vous permet de vivre avec vue sur le Times Square. Les chambres sont originales et pratiques, souvent avec les lits en étage pour une utilisation optimale de l'espace. Le sauna et la chambre à vapeur vous permettent de vous détendre. Dans le « Mezzanine Lounge » au bar et à la piscine, il y a une atmosphère conviviale.

El hotel, de propriedad de André Balazs, brinda la oportunidad de alojarse con una vista sobre el Times Square. Las habitaciones están amuebladas con un estilo original e práctico, muchas de ellas con literas para una utilización óptima del espacio. Posee sauna y baño de vapor en los que relajarse, bar y piscina y el "Mezzanine Lounge" para relacionarse.

Di proprietà di André Balazs, l'hotel offre la possibilità di alloggiare con vista su Times Square. Le camere sono arredate in stile originale e pratico, molte con letti a castello per un uso ottimale dello spazio. Per il relax ci sono la sauna e il bagno di vapore, e per chi vuole socializzare ci sono il "Mezzanine Lounge", il bar e la piscina.

Night Hotel

132 West 45th Street
New York, NY 10036
Times Square
Phone: +1 / 212 / 8 35 96 00
Fax: +1 / 212 / 8 35 96 10
www.nighthotelny.com

Prices: Double room from $ 340, Penthouse Suite $ 2 500
Services: Yoga, meditation in the Chopra Center
Public transportation: 1, 2, 3, 7, N, Q, R, S, W 42 Street-Times Square
Map: No. 40

Located in the center of New York's colorful Theater District, this hotel has a consistent black-and-white design. The concept extends to the bathrooms and modern flat-screen TVs. In addition, there are long, glass-covered corridors, subdued light, and sparkling chrome: it's always night at the Night Hotel, even when the sun streams in.

Cet hôtel situé en plein centre du quartier animé des théâtres est décoré de manière conséquente en noir et blanc. Ce concept s'étend aussi aux salles de bain et aux écrans plats des téléviseurs modernes. On y trouve aussi de longs corridors aux plafond vitrés, de la lumière discrète, du chrome brillant : dans le Night Hotel, il fait toujours nuit, même quand le soleil brille partout.

Ubicado en el centro del variopinto distrito teatral de Nueva York, este hotel es todo en blanco y negro. El concepto se repite hasta en los baños y en los modernos televisores de pantalla plana. Además hay largos pasillos con bóvedas de cristal, iluminación discreta, cromo centelleante: en el Night Hotel siempre es de noche, aunque sea inundado por la luz del sol.

Situato nel centro del variopinto quartiere teatrale di New York, questo hotel punta decisamente sul bianco e nero. Il concetto si estende ai bagni e ai moderni televisori a schermo piatto. In più ci sono lunghi corridoi dalle volte in vetro, luci discrete, cromo scintillante: nel Night Hotel è sempre notte, anche quando il sole lo inonda della sua luce.

THE TIME Hotel

224 West 49th Street
New York, NY 10019
Times Square
Phone: +1 / 212 / 2 46 52 52
Fax: +1 / 212 / 2 45 23 05
www.thetimeny.com

Prices: Double room $ 179 to $ 609, suite $ 339 to $ 739
Public transportation: 1, C, E 50 Street; N, R, W 49 Street
Map: No. 50

THE TIME Hotel has a clear structure. Rooms are cozy and furnished with gentle effects. Adam D. Tihany designed them in the three primary colors of red, yellow, and blue, which the guest can experience with all the senses. This unusual color concept is applied consistently from the beds to the candy.

THE TIME Hotel a une structure claire, les chambres sont confortables et arrangées avec des effets doux. Adam D. Tihany a conçu l'intérieur dans les trois couleurs primaires rouge, jaune et bleu, que le visiteur peut laisser agir sous tous ses sens. Ce concept de couleurs inhabituel s'étend des lits jusqu'aux bonbons.

THE TIME Hotel tiene una estructura clara, las habitaciones son confortables y amuebladas con toques suaves, diseñadas por Adam D. Tihany en los tres colores primarios: el rojo, amarillo y azul, que se dejan absorber a través de todos los sentidos. Este concepto cromático poco común sigue repitiéndose desde las camas hasta ... en los caramelos.

THE TIME Hotel ha una struttura limpida, le camere sono confortevoli e arredate con effetti gentili, disegnate da Adam D. Tihany nei tre colori primari rosso, giallo e azzurro, che l'ospite può sperimentare con tutti i propri sensi. Questo concetto cromatico poco abituale si ripete con coerenza, dai letti fino alle caramelle.

Dream New York

210 West 55th Street
New York, NY 10019
Midtown
Phone: +1 / 212 / 2 47 20 00
Fax: +1 / 646 / 7 56 20 88
www.dreamny.com

Prices: From $ 229
Public transportation: B, D, E Seventh Avenue; N, Q, R, W
57 Street; 1 50 Street
Map: No. 16

The Dream New York is a multicultural oasis: the restaurant offers Italian-inspired cuisine, the "Dream Lounge" invites guests to flirt, and a second lounge in a style inspired by the French Riviera allows a marvelous view from the roof terrace. You can relax at the Spa Center with its Far Eastern flair.

Le Dream New York est une oasis multiculturelle : le restaurant offre de la cuisine d'inspiration italienne, le « Dream Lounge », invite à flirter et un deuxième foyer dans le style de la Côte d'Azur française offre une vue superbe depuis la terrasse sur le toit. Vous pouvez vous détendre dans un centre de bains d'inspiration est-asiatique.

El Dream New York es un oasis multicultural: el restaurante ofrece comida de inspiración italiana, el "Dream Lounge" invita al ligue y otro salón con una decoración inspirada al estilo de la Costa Francesa permite una magnifica vista desde el mirador del techo. Para relajarse hay un centro spa con gusto asiático.

Il Dream New York è un'oasi multiculturale: il ristorante offre cucina di ispirazione italiana, il "Dream Lounge" invita al flirt e una seconda sala in stile ispirato alla riviera francese permette una vista grandiosa dalla terrazza sul tetto. È possibile rilassarsi all'interno del centro termale dal sapore asiatico.

Chambers

15 West 56th Street
New York, NY 10019
Midtown
Phone: +1 / 212 / 9 74 56 56
Fax: +1 / 212 / 9 74 56 57
www.chambershotel.com

Prices: Single room from $ 295, double room from $ 450, suite from $ 850
Services: Direct high-speed Internet access, CD/DVD players and library, complimentary passes to New York Sports Club
Public transportation: F 57 Street
Map: No. 12
Editor's tip: Personal shoppers at luxury store Henri Bendel are available to guests.

The Chambers combines a rather coarse design charm with the classical furnishing style of a modern town house. Located close to the MoMA, it also looks like a private art gallery: 500 originals by various famous artists are distributed throughout the 14 floors of the building. The "Town" restaurant offers exquisite French cuisine.

Le Chambers combine un charme design plutôt rigoureux avec le style de l'intérieur d'une maison urbaine moderne. Situé près du MoMA, il ressemble lui-même à une galerie d'art privée : 500 originaux de divers grands artistes sont répartis sur les 14 étages de la maison. Le testaurant « Town » offre de la cuisine française exquise.

El diseño del Chambers une un encanto austero y un mobiliario clásico con el estilo de una moderna casa de ciudad. Ubicado cerca del MoMa, el mismo hotel es toda una galería de arte privada: 500 obras originales de artistas famosos enriquecen las 14 plantas del edificio. El restaurante "Town" ofrece una excelente comida francesa.

Il design del Chambers unisce un certo fascino ruvido con l'arredamento in stile classico di una moderna casa di città. Situato nei pressi del MoMA, l'hotel stesso è praticamente una galleria d'arte privata: 500 opere originali di famosi artisti sono distribuite sui 14 piani dell'edificio. Il ristorante "Town" offre una succulenta cucina francese.

Four Seasons Hotel

57 East 57th Street
New York, NY 10022
Midtown
Phone: +1 / 212 / 7 58 57 00
Fax: +1 / 212 / 75 85 71
www.fourseasons.com

Prices: Double room from $ 595
Services: Fully equipped Business Center, 465 m² Fitness Center and Spa, children's amenities, babysitting services
Public transportation: 4, 5, 6 59 Street-Lexington Avenue; N, R, W Fifth Avenue-59 Street
Map: No. 20

Many people think that the Four Seasons, designed by star architect I.M. Pei, is the finest luxury hotel in New York. Its spacious, elegantly furnished rooms often offer a view across Central Park. The trendy "FiftySeven" restaurant is classy but not too expensive. Its bar occasionally hosts after-work parties.

Pour beaucoup, le Four Seasons, conçu par l'architecte « Star » I.M. Pei est l'hôtel de luxe le plus noble à New York. Ses chambres généreuses avec les meubles élégants offrent souvent une vue sur Central Park. Le restaurant branché « FiftySeven » a de la class sans être trop cher. Des fois, il ya des soirées organisées au bar.

Obra del famoso arquitecto I.M. Pei, es para muchos el hotel de lujo más noble de Nueva York. Muchas de las habitaciones, amplias y elegantes, tienen vista al Central Park. El nombrado restaurante "FiftySeven" aún siendo de lujo, no es demasiado caro. En el bar son habituales las fiestas a la salida del trabajo.

Il Four Seasons, progettato dal celebre architetto I.M. Pei, è da molti ritenuto il più pregiato tra gli hotel di lusso di New York. Le camere sono spaziose ed eleganti, molte di esse con vista sul Central Park. Il ristorante "FiftySeven" è lussuoso e alla moda, e tuttavia non troppo caro. Il bar ospita talvolta party dopolavoro.

The Lowell Hotel

28 East 63rd Street
New York, NY 10021
Upper East Side
Phone: +1 / 212 / 8 38 14 00
Fax: +1 / 212 / 3 19 42 30
www.lowellhotel.com

Prices: Single room from $ 545, double room from $ 635, suite $ 1 265
Services: 33 rooms with wood-burning fireplaces, 14 suites with terraces, special services for children and pets
Public transportation: F Lexington Avenue-63 Street; N, R, W Fifth Avenue-59 Street; 4, 5, 6 59 Street
Map: No. 31

This small but fine hotel in the heart of New York offers a rustic atmosphere in the middle of the metropolis and belongs to the "Leading Hotels of the World". The 23 deluxe rooms and 47 suites are furnished in an individual, cozy, and stylish way. The restaurant "The Post House" is one of the ten best steakhouses in America.

Ce petit hôtel noble au cœur de New York offre une atmosphère rustique au milieu de la métropole et compte parmi les « Leading Hotels of the World ». Les 23 chambres de luxe et les 47 suites ont du style et sont individuelles et confortables. Le restaurant « The Post House » compte parmi les dix meilleures maisons du steak en Amérique.

Pequeño pero refinado hotel en el corazón de Nueva York, brinda una atmósfera rural en el medio de la metrópolis, es uno de los "Leading Hotels of the World". El estilo de las 23 habitaciones deluxe y 47 suites es característico, confortable y con gusto. "The Post House" es uno de los diez mejores asadores de América.

Questo piccolo e raffinato hotel nel cuore di New York offre un'atmosfera rustica in mezzo alla metropoli, ed è uno dei "Leading Hotels of the World". Le 23 camere deluxe e le 47 suite presentano uno stile individuale, confortevole e di buon gusto. Il ristorante "The Post House" è tra le dieci migliori steakhouse d'America.

Plaza Athénée

37 East 64th Street
New York, NY 10021
Upper East Side
Phone: +1 / 212 / 7 34 91 00
Fax: +1 / 212 / 7 72 09 58
www.plaza-athenee.com

Prices: Double room from $ 695, suite from $ 1 470
Public transportation: F Lexington Avenue-63 Street;
N, R, W Fifth Avenue-59 Street; 4, 5, 6 59 Street
Map: No. 43

This hotel icon on the Upper East Side is modeled after a distinguished European Grand Hotel. The house provides sophisticated elegance, calm but highly efficient service, and comfortable, spacious rooms—which the many regulars appreciate. In addition, it offers in-room massages and other amenities.

Cet icône d'hôtel sur le Upper East Side s'inspire d'un grand hôtel de classe à l'européenne. La maison offre une élégance sobre, un service discret mais très efficace et des chambres confortables et spacieuses – de nombreux clients habitués les apprécient. De plus, des massages en chambre et autres services de confort sont offerts.

El estilo de este hotel-icono en la Upper East Side se inspira en uno de los nobles grandes hoteles europeos. El edificio ofrece una elegancia de buen gusto, servicio inquebrantable pero muy eficiente y confortable, amplias habitaciones apreciadas por los numerosos clientes habituales. Proporciona además servicio de masaje en las habitaciones y otras amenidades.

Lo stile di questo hotel-icona sulla Upper East Side prende spunto da uno dei più rinomati Grand Hotel europei. L'edificio presenta un'eleganza di buon gusto, servizio imperturbabile ma efficiente e confortevole, camere spaziose che i numerosi clienti regolari sanno apprezzare. Offre inoltre un servizio di massaggio in camera e altre comodità.

What else?

New York is an amusement park that you can explore by land, water, or air. Attractive tours are a cruise on a sailing ship with the backdrop of Manhattan or a day trip on the water taxi. The green park oases in the city offer pleasant relaxation. Visits to the gigantic Bronx Zoo or Battery Park City with its diverse leisure-time possibilities are also worth seeing.

New York est un parc d'attractions que vous pouvez explorer par terre, sur l'eau ou dans l'air. A recommander : une croisière à la voile devant la silhouette de Manhattan ou un tour avec un des taxis à l'eau. Les oasis vertes des parcs dans la ville offrent un repos soulageant, une visite du Bronx Zoo ou de Battery Park City avec ses loisirs divers, cela vaut bien le prix du déplacement.

Nueva York es un parque de atracciones que se puede descubrir desde tierra, mar o aire. Muy excitantes son los paseos en barco de vela con Manhattan como escenario, así como las excursiones en el taxi acuático. Los verdes oasis de la ciudad ofrecen una placentera recuperación, igualmente gratificantes, son las visitas al colosal Zoo del Bronx o a Battery Park City con sus múltiples diversiones.

New York è come un parco dei divertimenti, che si può esplorare dalla terra, dall'acqua o dall'aria, ad esempio con un giro in barca a vela con Manhattan a fare da sfondo o una gita sul taxi acquatico. Le oasi verdi della città offrono un piacevole ristoro, e altrettanto fruttuosa sarà una visita al gigantesco zoo del Bronx o a Battery Park City con le sue svariate opportunità di svago.

Left page: Coney Island
Right page: Left Bronx Zoo, right Central Park

New York Water Taxi

Landings:
– South Street Seaport
– West 44th Street
– Fulton Ferry Landing
– Battery Park
Phone: +1 / 212 / 7 42 19 69
www.nywatertaxi.com

Opening hours: Year-round, special tours from April–Dec
Prices: Gateway to America tour $ 20, children (12 and under)
$ 12, "Hop On/Hop Off" pass (valid for two days) $ 25, children
$ 15, Sunset Happy Hour cruises from 7 pm to 8.30 pm for 21
and over $ 20. It is recommended that you purchase tickets in
advance at www.nywatertaxi.com.
Map: No. 39

During the one-hour "Gateway to America" tour in the water taxi, you will learn many things about the time period beginning with the first settlements of the Native Americans, the immigrant era, and up to the attacks of September 11. You can explore New York for two days on your own route with the "Hop On/Hop Off" pass.

Pendant le tour d'une heure « Gateway to America » dans le taxi d'eau, vous apprenez beaucoup sur les premières colonies des indigènes et les temps des immigrants jusqu'aux attaques du 11 septembre. Avec le passeport « Hop On/Hop Off », vous pouvez explorer New York pendant deux jours en suivant votre propre parcours.

La excursión "Gateway to America" por el dique del puerto de Nueva York dura una hora y permite aprender mucho sobre los primeros nativos americanos, desde los tiempos de la colonización, hasta el ataque del 11 de Septiembre. Utilizando un solo pase "Hop On/Hop Off" se puede admirar Nueva York durante dos días eligiendo libremente las rutas a recorrer.

Durante l'escursione "Gateway to America" sul taxi acquatico, della durata di un'ora, si può apprendere molto sui primi insediamenti dei nativi americani, sull'epoca dell'immigrazione, giù fino all'attacco dell'11 settembre. Con il pass "Hop On/Hop Off" è possibile esplorare New York per due giorni scegliendo il proprio itinerario.

NEW YORK WATER TAXI

Bryant Park

500 Fifth Avenue
New York, NY 10110
Midtown
Phone: +1 / 212 / 7 68 42 42
www.bryantpark.org

Opening hours: Daily, park will be closed in the evenings
Specials: Free wireless Internet access in the entire park
Public transportation: F, V, B, D 42 Street-Bryant Park;
7 Fifth Avenue
Map: No. 8

Named after poet and newspaper publisher William Cullen Bryant, the park—after phases as a hippie hangout and terrain of dealers and the homeless—was redesigned and reopened in 1992. Now there are festivals here and it is also a favorite place for family outings and rendezvous.

Ce parc, nommé d'après le poète et éditeur de presse William Cullen Bryant, a été, – après des phases comme point de rencontre « hippie » et terrain pour des dealers et sans-abris – refaçonné et rouvert en 1992. Aujourd'hui, des festivals sont organisés ici et c'est un endroit très apprécié pour des randonnées de famille et des rendez-vous.

El parque recibe su nombre por el poeta y editor de periódicos William Cullen Bryant y fue reformado y reabierto en 1992, tras haber sido un punto de encuentro para hippies y refugio para traficantes y desamparados. Hoy en día es lugar festivales, y un punto favorito para excursiones familiares y citas.

Il parco prende il nome dal poeta ed editore giornalistico William Cullen Bryant ed è stato riorganizzato e riaperto nel 1992, dopo aver attraversato fasi di ritrovo per hippy e di rifugio per spacciatori e senzatetto. Oggi vi si tengono festival ed è un luogo prediletto per gite di famiglia e appuntamenti.

Central Park

From 59 Street in the South to 110 Street in the North, from Fifth Avenue in the East to Eighth Avenue in the West
www.centralpark.com

Opening hours: Daily 6 am to 1 am
Public transportation: 4, 5, 6 along Fifth Avenue; A, B, C along Eighth Avenue
Map: No. 10

New York's biggest natural facility is 2.5 miles long and about half a mile wide—almost twice as large as the Principality of Monaco. It was handed over to the public in 1873. Encircled by high-rises, the charming park is perfectly designed any time of the year with details such as cast-iron bridges.

Avec une longueur de 4 km et une largeur de presque 1 km, le plus grand parc naturel de New York — ouvert au public en 1873 — est deux fois plus grand que la Principauté de Monaco. Entouré de gratte-ciels, ce parc, qui est beau pendant chaque saison, est parfaitement conçu jusqu'aux détails comme les ponts en fonte.

El área verde más grande de Nueva York, entregado al público en 1873, mide 4 km de largo por casi 1 km de ancho, el doble del Principado de Mónaco. Rodeado por altas construcciones, mantiene el encanto en todas las épocas del año y está perfectamente cuidado en todos sus detalles, como puentes de hierro labrado.

La maggiore area verde di New York, donata al pubblico nel 1873, misura 4 km di lunghezza per quasi 1 km di larghezza — il doppio del Principato di Monaco. Circondato da alti edifici, è ricco di fascino in tutte le stagioni, ed è perfettamente curato fin nei dettagli, come ponti in ferro battuto.

Fort Tryon Park / The Cloisters

Fort Tryon Park
New York, NY 10040
Upper Manhattan
Phone: +1 / 212 / 9 23 37 00
Museum: +1 / 212 / 6 50 22 80
www.metmuseum.org

Opening hours: Nov–Feb Tue–Sun 9.30 am to 5 pm, March–Oct to 5.30 pm
Prices: $ 20, students, senior citizens $ 10, children (12 and under) free
Public transportation: A 190 Street, Bus M4 to Fort Tryon Park / The Cloisters
Map: No. 19
Editor's tip: You can visit The Metropolitan Museum of Art with the entry ticket to The Cloisters on the same day!

Built beginning in 1934, original architectural fragments from French and Spanish monasteries and churches were used for The Cloisters. A portion of the medieval collection of the Met is exhibited here: sculptures, paintings, illuminated manuscripts, the works of goldsmiths and silversmiths, glass, and ivory. The attached park is also beautiful.

Construit à partir de 1934, The Cloisters (Les Cloîtres) comporte des fragments architecturaux en provenance de cloîtres français et espagnols. Une partie de la collection médiévale du Met est exposée ici : des sculptures, peintures, manuscrits illuminés, ouvrages en or et argent, verre et ivoire. Le parc associé est également très beau.

Para construir The Cloisters, a partir de 1934, se emplearon fragmentos arquitectónicos de iglesias y monasterios franceses y españoles. Parte de la colección del Met se expone aquí: esculturas, cuadros, manuscritos iluminados, obras de orfebrería y platería, trabajos en cristal y en marfil. También maravilloso el parque adyacente.

Per la costruzione dei Cloisters, iniziata nel 1934, si impiegarono frammenti architettonici originali di chiese e monasteri francesi e spagnoli. Una parte della collezione medievale del Met è qui esposta: sculture, dipinti, manoscritti illuminati, opere d'oreficeria e argenteria, lavori in vetro e in avorio. Magnifico anche il parco adiacente.

Coney Island

Surf Avenue
Brooklyn, NY 11224
Coney Island
www.coneyisland.com

Opening hours: Beach and promenade are open all year round; rides and attractions are open from Easter until the end of September
Public transportation: D, F, N, Q Stillwell Avenue
Map: No. 13
Editor's tip: "Nathan's Famous" (corner Surf Ave / Stillwell Ave) has the best hot-dogs in town. The annual hot dog eating contest is held here on July 4th at noon.

The 3-mile long beach of Coney Island was already a popular day-trip destination for families and lovers 100 years ago. There is an amusement park, countless fast-food stands (the hot dog was supposedly invented here), and artificial palms. The aquarium with its dolphins is also an attraction.

Il y a 100 ans, la plage de Coney Island, d'une longueur de 5 km, était déjà une destination populaire pour des familles et des amoureux. On trouve ici un champ de foire, de nombreux snack-bars – on dit que le « Hot Dog » a été inventé ici – et des palmiers artificiels. L'aquarium avec ses dauphins est une attraction.

Desde hace 100 años la playa de Coney Island, larga 5 km, es el destino para excursiones familiares y enamorados. Posee un parque de atracciones, gran cantidad de puestos de comida rápida (se cuenta que aquí nacieron los perritos calientes), palmeras artificiales y un acuario con delfines.

La spiaggia di Coney Island, lunga 5 km, già 100 anni fa era una meta di escursioni prediletta da famiglie e innamorati. Vi si trova il parco dei divertimenti, innumerevoli bancarelle di fast-food (a quanto pare qui fu inventato l'hot dog) e palme artificiali. Tra le attrazioni, l'acquario con i suoi delfini.

Bronx Zoo

Bronx River Parkway, Exit 6
Pehlam Parkway / Boston Road
Bronx, NY 10460
Phone: +1 / 718 / 3 67 10 10
www.bronxzoo.com

Opening hours: Nov–March 10 am to 4.30 pm, April–Oct 10 am to 5 pm, Sat+Sun to 5.30 pm
Prices: $ 14, children (2–12 years) $ 10, senior citizens (65 and over) $ 12, Wed by donation (extremely busy), special entry fee for rides and attractions such as the Bug Carousel
Public transportation: 2, 5 East Tremont Avenue-West Farms Square
Map: No. 5

The largest urban zoo in the USA covers an area equivalent to about 150 soccer fields. More than 4,000 animals roam here. A special highlight is the Congo Gorilla Forest, but the other enclosures are also close to nature and have an excellent design. The zoo is also known for its nature-conservation activities.

Le plus grand parc zoologique aux Etats-Unis couvre une superficie de 150 terrains de football. Il y a plus de 4000 animaux ici. Une attraction spéciale est la Forêt des Gorilles du Congo mais d'autres enclos sont aussi bien conçus de manière naturelle. Les activités du zoo en matière de protection naturelle sont largement connues.

Es el zoo de ciudad más grande de los Estados Unidos, equivale a 150 campos de fútbol y es el reino de más de 4000 animales. Destaca la Selva de los Gorilas del Congo, pero hay más ambientes perfectamente creados como en la realidad. Son muy conocidas sus actividades de conservación de la naturaleza.

Il più grosso zoo cittadino degli Stati Uniti occupa un'area equivalente a circa 150 campi da calcio, e vi scorrazzano oltre 4000 animali. Spicca la Foresta dei Gorilla del Congo, ma diversi altri recinti sono fedelmente ricostruiti come in natura. Sono inoltre ben note le attività di conservazione della natura dello zoo.

Staten Island Botanical Garden

1000 Richmond Terrace
Staten Island, NY 10301
Staten Island
Phone: +1 / 718 / 2 73 82 00
www.sibg.org

Opening hours: Sunrise to sunset
Prices: Generally free; New York Chinese Scholar's Garden:
$5, children (12 and under) $ 4; Connie Gretz's Secret Garden:
adults $ 2
Public transportation: 1 South Ferry; R, W Whitehall;
4, 5 Bowling Green; then from ferry terminal ramp D bus route
S40 to Snug Harbor
Map: No. 47

The garden is arranged according to the ancient Chinese tradition—its model was the era of the Han Dynasty in China about 2,000 years ago. A landscape with many trees and small buildings stretches behind the enormous palace. Also worth seeing: the wonderfully ornamented old wall and the rare variety of orchids.

Le jardin est conçu selon l'ancienne tradition chinoise-de l'époque de la dynastie Han en Chine il y a environ 2000 ans. Derrière l'énorme palais, il y a un paysage boisé avec des constructions raffinées. A voir aussi la vieux mur merveilleusement décoré et une variété rare d'orchidées.

El jardín es mantenido según la antigua tradición china, tal como se hacía hace 2000 años en la dinastía Han. En el interior del majestuoso palacio se extiende un paisaje de árboles y pequeños edificios. También se pueden admirar la magníficamente adornada antigua muralla y las raras variedades de orquídeas.

Il giardino è disposto secondo l'antica tradizione cinese, sul modello dell'epoca della dinastia Han di 2.000 anni fa circa. Dietro all'imponente palazzo si estende un paesaggio di macchie arboree e piccoli edifici sparsi. Da vedere anche l'antico muro, magnificamente adornato, e le rare varietà di orchidea.

ARRIVAL IN NEW YORK

By Plane

There are direct flights from various European cities to the airports John F. Kennedy International Airport and Newark Liberty International Airport. The La Guardia Airport is mainly serving domestic air traffic.

Further information on the airports: www.panynj.gov

John F. Kennedy International Airport (JFK)
Phone: +1 / 718 / 2 44 44 44
JFK is situated in Queens, approx. 24 km (15 miles) from Midtown Manhattan. After passing customs and baggage claim, follow the Ground Transportation signs to continue your travel into the city. Off-peak travel times range between 40 and 60 mins by cab or bus. With the SuperShuttle bus you can reach any address as well as all hotels in Manhattan. Buses depart at least every 20 mins and a single trip costs $ 13–22. You can register for the trip into the city at the Ground Transportation Desk, reservations for return trips should be made 24 hrs in advance, Phone: +1 / 212 / 2 58 38 26 or +1 / 800 / 258 38 26, www.supershuttle.com. The buses of the New York Airport Service go to Manhattan (Grand Central Station, Port Authority Bus Terminal, Penn Station), single trip $ 15, Phone: +1/212 / 8 75 82 00, www.nyairportservice.com. Trips by Air Train and Subway are more complicated and also take longer: change trains at the subway station Howard Beach to subway A or at Jamaica Station to subway E, J, Z or to the Long Island Rail Road. Total travel times range between 70 and 90 mins, single trip approx. $ 12, you can only carry a limited amount of baggage. Cabs to Midtown Manhattan are $ 45 fixed price plus charges for bridges and tunnels as well as tips. Only use licensed yellow cabs!

Newark Liberty International Airport (EWR)
Phone: +1 / 973 / 9 61 60 00
This airport is situated approx. 26 km (16 miles) from Midtown Manhattan in New Jersey and less complex than JFK. After customs and baggage claim, follow the Ground Transportation signs to continue your trip into the city, off-peak travel times range between 40 and 60 mins. Bus transfer with SuperShuttle (see above for reservation and pricing information) or with Newark Liberty Airport Express every 15–30 mins to Manhattan (Port Authority Bus Terminal, Bryant Park, Grand Central Station), single trip $ 14, Phone: +1 / 800 / 6 69 00 51, www.coachusa.com. More complicated is traveling by Air Train or normal trains: change trains at Newark Liberty International Airport Train Station to NJ Transit or Amtrak direction Penn Station, single trip approx. $ 12. Cabs to Midtown Manhattan, $ 40–60 plus road charge and tips as well as additional charges for rush hour or weekends, if applicable.

Flight Safety
There are strict safety requirements for hand luggage, e.g. for carrying liquids. The Transport Security Administration is authorized to open travelers' luggage without their permission, if necessary by force. Therefore, do not lock your luggage. Furthermore, custom authorities are allowed to check computers and data storage media without the necessity of concrete suspicious facts. For information on current regulations visit the website of the US embassy www.tsa.gov.

Immigration and Customs Regulations

Travel documents: Travelers need to have the correct travel documents and visas if necessary. Visas can be applied for at the American Consulate based in the country of origin.
Border control: On check-in travelers already have to present either a booking confirmation for their hotel or provide details concerning the location of their initial accommodation. When entering the US, electronic fingerprints as well as an electronic portrait photo are taken from all visitors. Furthermore, you may be asked about your return ticket, the motivation for your trip and/or your domicile during your stay.
Customs: Adults 21 years and older are allowed to bring in 200 cigarettes or 50 cigars or 2 kg of tobacco as well as 1 l of alcohol and presents amounting to a value of $ 100. The import of comestibles is prohibited.

INFORMATION

Tourist Information

NYC & Company
810 Seventh Avenue
New York, NY 10019
Phone: +1 / 212 / 4 84 12 00
Fax: +1 / 212 / 2 45 59 43
www.nycvisit.com
Mon–Fri 8.30 am to 6 pm, Sat+Sun 8.30 am to 5 pm. Visitor Information Center branch offices:

NYC Heritage Tourism Center
Corner Broadway/Park Row, south of City Hall Park. Mon–Fri 9 am to 6 pm, Sat+Sun 10 am to 6 pm
Official Visitor Information Kiosk Chinatown
Corner Canal/Walker/Baxter Street
Sun–Fri 10 am to 6 pm, Sat 10 am to 7 pm

City Magazines
New York's most popular city magazine is **Village Voice**. It provides in-scene news and is published every Wed. It is available for free in many shops and clubs as well as in special boxes on the pavements. **Time Out New York** and **New York Magazine** are available every Wed respectively Mon at newspaper stands and offer a broad schedule of events, restaurant reviews, party recommendations and many more. The **New Yorker** is known for providing elaborate background essays. Furthermore, you can find information on current events in the supplements of the **New York Times.**

Websites

General
www.nyc.gov – Official site of New York City
www.nytimes.com – Web presence of the "New York Times", with news about the city, event calendar, online ticket service, restaurant search engine, cinema program, tips for travelers and many more

Going Out
City magazines and online travel guides offer information on restaurants, taverns, bars, events and many more on the Internet
http://newyork.citysearch.com
http://nymag.com
www.ny.com
www.timeoutny.com
www.villagevoice.com

Art and Culture
www.broadway.com – Program of Broadway shows
www.newyorker.com – Comprehensive art and culture program

www.nytheatre.com – Everything about the New York theater scene

Sports and Leisure
www.chelseapiers.com – Leisure and sport facility
www.nycgovparks.org – Sport and leisure time facilities in all parks of the city
www.skatecity.com/nyc – Skating in New York, with travel routes and maps

Map
www.newyork.citysam.de – Interactive city maps

Accommodation
www.1800usahotels.com/nycvisit/index.html – Hotel agency of the tourist information
http://newyork.citysearch.com – Online travel guide, hotel reservation etc.
www.nyhabitat.com – This site helps you to find apartments and Bed & Breakfast accommodations

Event calendars
www.nycvisit.com
http://newyork.citysearch.com
http://nymag.com

RECOMMENDED LITERATURE

Paul Auster
The New York Trilogy: "City of Glass", "Ghosts" and "Locked Room". Three elaborately constructed mystery fiction novels that describe the anonymity of big city life, the decay of social relationships and the loss of moral order.

Truman Capote
Breakfast at Tiffany's. The story of the mysteri-ous, innocently wicked Holly Golightly, who is trying to find her luck in New York.

John Dos Passos
Manhattan Transfer. Multi-facetted picture of the New York of the early 20ies, where the pursuit of work, happiness and power is predominant.

F. Scott Fitzgerald
The Great Gatsby. One of the classics of American literature – a portrait of New York's monied nobility in the Roaring Twenties.

Tom Wolfe
The Bonfire of the Vanities. Tragical-comical big-city novel about the Wall Street generation.

CITY TOURS

Sightseeing Tours

By Bus and Subway
An inexpensive way of seeing Manhattan is a trip with the **M 1 bus** from E 8th Street/4th Avenue (Mon–Fri also from South Ferry) to W 146th Street in Harlem and back. A trip with the **subway** to see the subterranean Manhattan is always worthwhile – not only when it is raining.

Gray Line
Phone: +1 / 800 / 6 69 00 51 and +1 / 212 / 4 45 08 48
www.graylinenewyork.com
The All Loops Tours have four different routes through Manhattan and Brooklyn with the red double-decker buses. The bus stops on demand at one of the 50 stops. A trip lasts between 2 and 3 hrs and buses depart every 30 mins at Times Square for **Downtown Loop** and the **Holiday Lights Tour**, from Gray Line Visitors

Center (777 8th Avenue) for **Uptown Loop** and from South Street Seaport for the **Brooklyn Loop**. 48-hour ticket $ 44.

Boat Tours

Staten Island Ferry
A trip with the free ferry to Staten Island and back offers a great view on the Manhattan skyline and the Statue of Liberty. The ferry terminal is situated on Whitehall Street at the southern tip of Manhattan and ferries are leaving at least every 30 mins, duration of a single trip approx. 25 mins.

Circle Line
Phone: +1 / 212 / 5 63 32 00
www.circleline42.com
Boat trips of 75 mins and 2 hrs duration around the southern tip of Manhattan Island as well as a 3-hour island round trip. Departure from Pier 83 at the west end of 42nd Street. In summer various times a day, in winter less departures. Tickets $ 19, 24 and 29.

Sightseeing Flights

Helicopter round trips around the Statue of Liberty and over Downtown Manhattan. Flight times ranging between approx. 5–7 mins up to 30 mins, starting from $ 69/pers. Trial flight from 2 to 2.5 mins, $ 30/pers. Starting points: VIP Heliport (W 30th Street/ 12th Avenue), Downtown Manhattan Heliport (Pier 6 between South Street Seaport and Staten Island Ferry Terminal, Mon–Sat) and Paulus Hook Pier (Jersey City).

Helicopter Tours, Phone: +1 / 212 / 3 55 08 01
www.heliny.com
Liberty Helicopter Tours, Phone: +1 / 212 / 9 67 64 64 and +1 / 800 / 5 42 99 33

www.libertyhelicopters.com

Guided City Tours

Big Apple Greeter
1 Centre Street, 19th Floor, New York, NY 10007
Phone: +1 / 212 / 6 69 81 59
www.bigapplegreeter.org
People from New York provide a free guided tour for visitors through their city (max. 6 persons), duration 2 to 4 hrs. Registration via Internet, approx. 3–4 weeks in advance.

Big Onion Walking Tours
Phone: +1 / 212 / 4 39 10 90
www.bigonion.com
Competently guided walkabouts concentrating on special aspects and topics, e.g. immigration, gangs, etc., $ 15/pers.

Bike the Big Apple
Phone: +1 / 877 / 8 65 00 78
www.bikethebigapple.com
Guided bike tours through New York, duration 5–7 hours, length 8–15 miles, $ 65–75/pers. incl. bike and helmet.

Harlem Heritage Tours
Phone: +1 / 212 / 2 80 78 88
www.harlemheritage.com
Thematic walkabouts through Harlem (e.g. about the city's history, gospel churches) as well as special musical tours (Salsa, Hip-Hop, Jazz), from $ 25/pers.

Insight Seeing
Phone: +1 / 718 / 4 47 16 45
www.insightseeing-tours.de
2- to 6-hour tours through Manhattan, Harlem, Bronx, Brooklyn, Queens and Staten Island, in English from € 19/pers. Furthermore, individual tours, minimum duration 2 hrs, € 66/hr.

Lookouts

Breathtaking views are offered to visitors of the Observation Deck of the **Empire State Builing** (www.esbnyc.com) and from the Top of the Rock at **Rockefeller Center** (see above). Enjoy terrific views on the skyline of Manhattan from the **Staten Island Ferry** (see above), from the pavement leading over the **Brooklyn Bridge** or from **Roosevelt Island Tram**, an aerial cable-way going over the East River (www.rioc.com). Virtual tours with unusual New York air per-spectives can be undertaken at the **NYSkyride Cinema** at the Empire State Building (www.skyride.com).

TICKETS & DISCOUNTS

Ticket Offices

Order tickets for nearly all concerts, culture and sport events online or via phone at: **Ticketmaster**, Phone: +1 / 212 / 3 07 71 71, www.ticketmaster.com, phone service Mon–Fri 9 am to 9 pm, Sat to 8 pm, Sun to 6 pm **Telecharge**, Phone: +1 / 212 / 2 39 62 00, www.telecharge.com, 24-hour service

TKTS Theatre Centers

Discount tickets with reductions of 25 %, 35 % and 50 % for Broadway and Off-Broadway shows, for dance performances and musicals. Only available for shows and performances that take place on the respective day itself or matinees on the following day. Payment in cash or with traveller's cheques, $ 3 service charge. All available tickets are announced via a display panel. www.tdf.org. Points of sale: **TKTS Booth Times Square**, W 47th Street/ Broadway, Mon, Wed–Sat 3 pm till 8 pm, Tue from 2 pm, Sun from 3 pm (evening shows), Wed and Sat 10 am till 2 pm, Sun 11 am till 3 pm (matinees).

TKTS Booth South Street Seaport, John Street/ Front Street, Mon–Sat 11 am to 6 pm, Sun to 3 pm (evening shows), tickets for matinees only available one day in advance (Tue, Fri, Sat).

Discounts

City Passport

50% entrance discount and no waiting times in the following locations: Empire State Building, MoMA, Guggenheim Museum and American Museum of Natural History as well as to a 2-hour Circle Line boat trip. Available at the Visitor Center, the participating companies or online at www.citypass.com, $ 53/pers.

Unlimited Ride MetroCard

Unlimited use of subway, Staten Island Railway and the city buses as well as discounts for some museums, restaurants and shops. Available amongst others at the Visitor Center, in hotels and at MetroCard vending machines, one-day ticket $ 7, one-week ticket $ 24.

GETTING AROUND IN NEW YORK

Local Public Transport

Metropolitan Transportation Authority (MTA)

Phone: +1 / 718 / 3 30 12 34
www.mta.info
The fastest way to get around in New York is the **Subway**. It operates on about 30 routes with high frequency around-the-clock. Staten Island is served by Staten Island Railway (SIR), Long Island by Long Island Rail Road (LIRR). Local trains stop at all stations, while the faster express trains only stop at the stations marked on the subway maps with white circles and ovals. In addition to the subway there is a dense **network of bus lines**. Buses commute from 6 am until about midnight

every 5–15 mins. A single ticket for subway or bus is $ 2, for express buses $ 5, multiple-ride tickets with the rechargeable MetroCard, unlimited rides with the Unlimited Ride MetroCard. Available amongst others in subway stations, MetroCard vending machines and kiosks, single tickets can also be bought from the bus driver (make sure you pay the exact amount as drivers do not return any change!). The network maps for the subways, trains and buses are available for download at the homepage of the Metropolitan Transportation Authority.

Cabs

Phone: +1 / 212 / 3 02 82 94
Going by cab is relatively cheap in New York: $ 2.50 basic charge for the first 1/3-mile, $ 0.40 for every further 1/5-mile or for every 2 mins in case of traffic jam. Furthermore, additional charges for night trips from 8 pm–6 am, trips during rush hour, tunnel and bridge tolls have to be paid if applicable as well as a tip of 15 %. Normally, cabs are stopped by waving with the hand. When a cab is available the number on the roof is lighted, ordering a cab by phone is unusual. Only use licensed cabs – the yellow ones, that all are equipped with a taxi meter. Non-licensed cabs, so-called *gypsy cabs* most often do not dispose of insurance and claim higher charges.

FESTIVALS & EVENTS

This is just an excerpt from the program for the year.

Lunar New Year Celebration

End of Jan/beginnings of Feb (at the first full moon after the 21st Jan), New Year's celebration in Chinatown with parades, dragon dances and fireworks (www.explorechinatown.com).

St. Patrick's Day Parade

Around the 17th March, grand parade on Fifth Avenue between 44th and 86th Street in honor of the Irish national saint (www.saintpatricksdayparade.com).

Great Five Boro Bike Tour

At the beginnings of May, 42-miles bike tour through five districts of New York, accompanied by a festival (www.bikenewyork.org).

Museum Mile Festival

Second Tue in June, free admission to the nine big museums on Fifth Avenue as well as a street festival with live bands and entertainment (www.museummilefestival.org).

Shakespeare in the Park

Mid June–beginnings of July, Shakespeare performances on the open-air stage of the Delacorte Theater at Central Park, free admission, always starting at 8.30 pm, tickets can be obtained on the day of the performance at the Public Theater in Lafayette Street (Phone: +1 / 212 / 5 39 86 50, www.publictheater.org).

Central Park Summer Stage

Mid June–Mid Aug, concerts, dance performances, movie screenings and lectures on a stage in the middle of the Central Park, various events per week, usually free admission (www.summerstage.org).

Downtown River to River Festival

Mid June–Sept, more than 500 cultural events in theaters and museums on squares and in parks in Lower Manhattan (www.rivertorivernyc.com).

Useful Tips & Addresses

Good Morning America Concert
Beginnings of July–end of Aug, first-class pop concerts on the Upper Terrace in Bryant Park, free admission, beginning 7 am! (www.bryantpark.org).

New York Philharmonic in the Park
Mid July, open-air concerts of the Philharmonic Orchestra in Central Park and other green places in the city, with final fireworks, starting in each case at 8 pm (www.newyorkphilharmonic.org).

Sept 11th Anniversary
11th Sept, commemoration for the victims of the terrorist attacks on the World Trade Center with concerts, exhibitions and light show.

Greenwich Village Halloween Parade
31st Oct, nocturnal costume and torch procession between Spring Street and 22nd Street (www.halloween-nyc.com).

ING New York Marathon
Beginnings of Nov, the biggest marathon in the world leads through the five districts of New York (www.nycmarathon.com).

Lighting of the Rockefeller Center Christmas Tree
30th Nov, illumination of the big Christmas fir tree on Rockefeller Plaza.

New Year's Eve Ball
31st Dec, giant party starting in the early evening at Times Square with the famous Ball Drop from the top of the building One Times Square at 11.59 pm (www.timessquarebid.org).

USEFUL NOTES

Electricity
Voltage 110 volt. For electrical appliances you will need an adaptor.

Money
National currency: US-Dollar ($)
1 Dollar ($) = 100 Cents (ct)
Exchange rates: (as of early 2007):
$ 1 = approx. € 0.80 or € 1 = approx. $ 1.30
Bank and credit cards: Credit cards and traveler's cheques are accepted nearly everywhere. With EC-/Maestro-Cards and pin number you can withdraw US dollars from bank machines with the blue Cirrus sign: pull the card through the card reader, enter your PIN-number and choose option "Withdrawal from Checking". Notes of 50 and 100 dollars are only changed reluctantly in shops.

Health Insurance
Medical consultations and hospital stays have to be paid right away. Because of the high costs for medical care, a travel health insurance is strongly recommended.

Emergency
Emergency Hotline: Phone: 911 (police, fire department)
Emergency Doctor: Phone: + 1 / 800 / 3 95 34 00
Hotline for Crime Victims: Phone: +1 / 212 / 5 77 77 77
New York Hotel Urgent Medical Service: Phone: +1 / 212 / 7 37 12 12 (24-hour service, the doctors come directly to the hotel)

Opening Hours
Banks: Normally Mon–Fri 9 am to 3.30 pm, often Thu or Fri to 6 pm.
Shops: There is no store closing law in the

USA. Many shops are opened 24/7. Big stores in Midtown are closed on Sun. Jewish shops, mainly on the Lower East Side, are closed from Fri afternoon until Sat night.
Museums: Usually opened Tue–Sun 10 am to 5 pm, often opened until the evening once a week.
Restaurants: Upscale restaurants 11.30 am to 2 pm for lunch and 6 pm to 10 pm for dinner. Many taverns and restaurants are opened all day through, some of them even around the clock.

Smoking
Smoking is prohibited in public buildings, cabs, public transport vehicles, restaurants and bars. At hotels smokers should ask for a smoking room.

When to go
There is no specific season for traveling to New York – you can go there all year long. Summers can be very hot and sultry though. In July and Aug temperatures often reach 28°C. In Jan and Feb blizzards are likely to occur.

Safety
Today, New York is regarded to be the safest city in the USA. Nevertheless, the usual pre-cautions should be taken. Especially around Times Square and other busy places, in Grand Central Station and at the Port Authority bus station pick pocketing can occur. At night you should avoid empty streets and parks. It is recommended to have a purse with about $ 20 ready, that you can give away without resistance in case of emergency. Subway lines N and R commuting between Downtown and Midtown are busy till late at night. It is recommended to wait in the off-hour waiting areas that are situated near the exits of the stations.

Telephone
Area Codes of New York: 212, 917, 646 (Manhattan) and 718, 347 (Brooklyn, Bronx, Queens, Staten Island). Dial 1 first
Within New York: 1 + area code + desired phone number
Calling from Abroad: +1 + desired phone number without 0
Calling from New York: country code + area code without 0 + desired phone number
Operator: national: dial 0, international: dial 00 (telephone exchange of distance and collect calls as well as in case of emergency)
Directory Assistance: Phone 411
Toll-free numbers:
1 + 800, 888, 866 or 877 + desired phone number. With a prepaid phone card you can also make international calls. The activation code is disclosed when calling the phone number on the card. Phone cards are available at newspaper kiosks or tourist information centers. Cell phones only work when they are equipped triband technology. You can hire a cell phone for the time of your stay in New York, e.g. at the airport.

Tipping
In the United States service employees mainly live from the tips they get. Waiters and cab drivers receive a minimum tip of 15 % of the invoice amount. Chambermaids, porters, shoeshine boys and wardrobe attendants expect a tip of $ 1–2.

Time
New York belongs to the Eastern Time Zone, so that the time shift amounts to minus five hours in relation to Greenwich Mean Time (GMT). From the beginnings of April to the end of Oct watches are set one hour ahead due to summer time.

NEW JERSEY

Holland Tunne

48

47